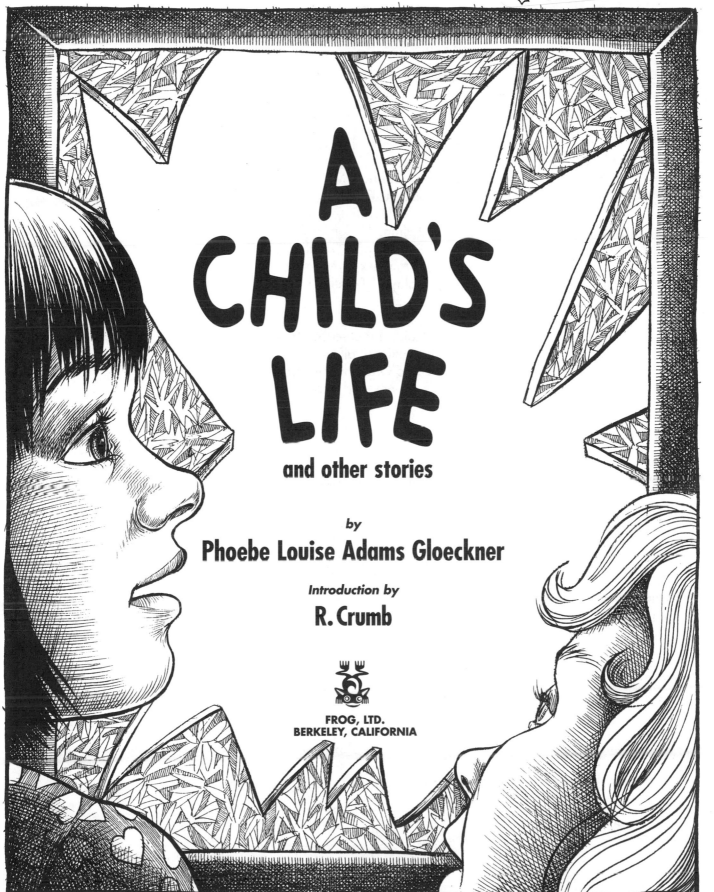

A CHILD'S LIFE

and other stories

by
Phoebe Louise Adams Gloeckner

Introduction by
R. Crumb

FROG, LTD.
BERKELEY, CALIFORNIA

ACKNOWLEDGMENTS

I want to thank the following people for the inspiration, encouragement and help they've given me:

J. Albertson, N. Auerbach, M. Adams, S. Beaupre, D. Bellamy, B. Botts, L. Calver, L. Cheney, R. Crumb, J. Fleming, W.J. "B." Griffith, A. Jones, A. Juno, J. Kalousek, K. Killian, A. Kominsky-Crumb, F. Andrew G., J. Goldenberg, T. Hann, S. Lafler, L. Lubeski, K. Milosevitch, J. Mindick, P. Mavrides, P. Muggia-Stuff, D. Noomin, B. Palay, V. Porter, Dr. S. Spotts, A. Suits, V. Vale.

And to Ayelet Maida for contributing to the design of the book and putting it all together, and to Lindy Hough and Richard Grossinger at Frog Ltd. for suggesting such a book and making it "happen."

Published by Frog, Ltd.

Frog, Ltd. books are distributed by
North Atlantic Books
P.O. Box 12327
Berkeley, CA 94712

Cover art by Phoebe Gloeckner
Pages 4 and 5 copyright © R. Crumb

Printed in the United States of America

Library of Congress Cataloging-in-Publication Data
Gloeckner, Phoebe
   A child's life : and other stories / Phoebe Gloeckner.
      p.   cm.
   ISBN 1-883319-71-4 (alk. paper)
   I. Title.
PN6727.G65C45   1998
741.5'973—dc21   97–47230
                                                      CIP

1 2 3 4 5 6 7 8 9 10 / 02 01 00 99 98

Stories and pictures have previously appeared in:

Mind Riot: Coming of Age in Comics, (Simon & Schuster, New York, NY, 1997): p. 88

BUZZARD, various issues & years (Cat-Head Comics, Hudson, MA): pp. 95, 96, 114, and 142.

Twisted Sisters II, (Kitchen Sink Press, Northampton, MA 1994): p. 70

WEIRDO, various issues & years (Last Gasp, San Francisco, CA): pp. 60, 65, and 66.

Wimmin's Comix, various issues and years (Rip Off Press, Auburn, CA (after 1987), Last Gasp, San Francisco, CA (pre-1987): pp. 55, 85, and 122.

Twisted Sisters, (Viking/Penguin, New York, NY, 1992): pp. 55, 60, 65, 117, and 122.

Young Lust #7, (Last Gasp, San Francisco, CA): pg. 117

The Atrocity Exhibition by J.G. Ballard, (RE/Search Publications, San Francisco, CA, 1990): pp. 126, 127, 128, 129, 138, 139, 140, and 141.

Angry Women, (RE/Search Publications, San Francisco, CA, 1991): p.132

Angry Women of Rock, (Juno Books, NYC, 1996): p.133

Future Sex Magazine, 1993: p.135

San Francisco Bay Guardian, 1995: p.54

CHAIN #2, (CHAIN, Buffalo, NY, 1995): p.66

Letters to the Author
Write: Phoebe Gloeckner, c/o Frog. Ltd, P.O. Box 12327, Berkeley, CA 94712
E-mail: phoebelouise@ravenblond.com
Website: http://www.ravenblond.com/pgloeckner

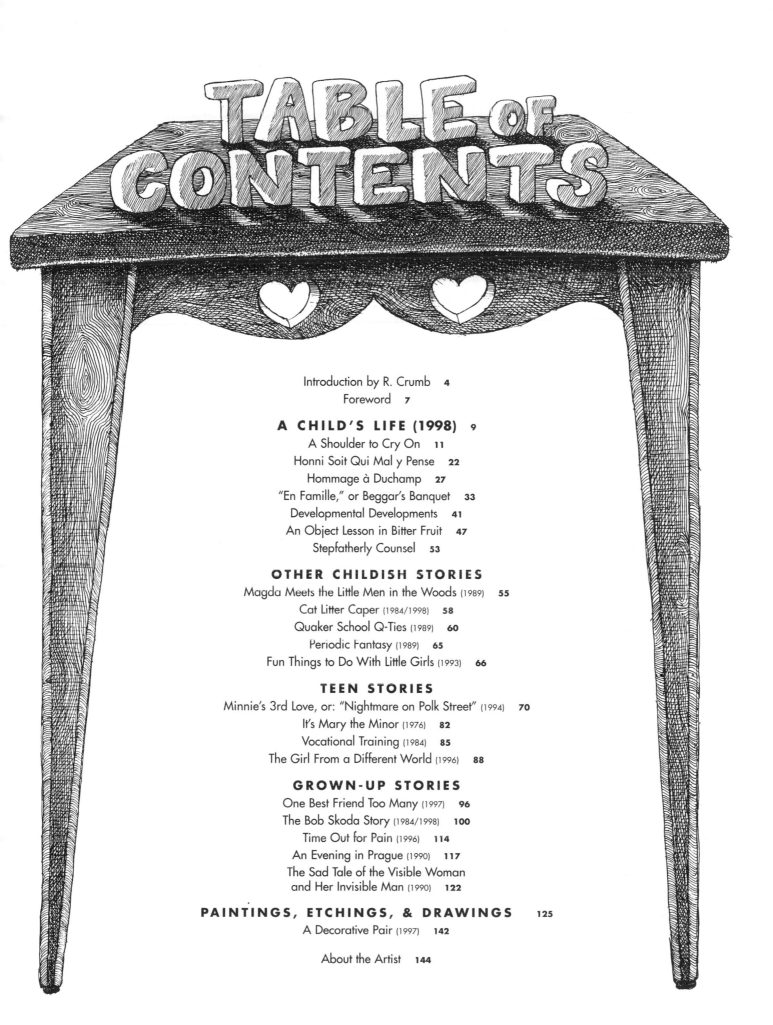

TABLE OF CONTENTS

PHOEBE

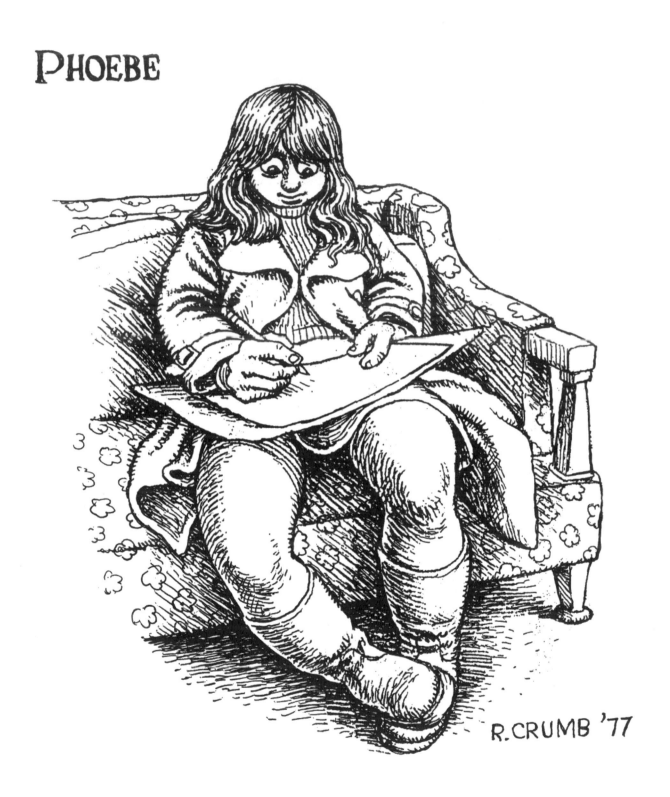

R. CRUMB '77

INTRODUCTION by R. CRUMB

PHOEBE ASKED ME IF I'D WRITE THIS INTRODUCTION AND I SAID, "SURE, BE HAPPY TO," AND I REALLY *WAS* HAPPY TO, BECAUSE I LOVE HER WORK, AND I'M GLAD THERE'S A BIG BOOK OF IT COMING OUT, BUT WHEN IT CAME TIME TO SIT DOWN AND *DO* IT, I HAD A HARD TIME. I HAVE TO TELL THE TRUTH. THE TRUTH IS THAT I'M JUST LIKE ALL THE OTHER DESPICABLE MALES THAT APPEAR IN THESE COMIC STORIES. I, TOO, LUSTED AFTER THE YOUNG, BUDDING ARTIST-CARTOONIST FROM THE MOMENT I FIRST MET HER, WHEN SHE WAS 16 OR 17 YEARS OLD. I, TOO, DESIRED TO SUBJECT THE BEAUTIFUL, INTENSE YOUNG GIRL TO ALL SORTS OF DEGRADING AND PERVERSE SEXUAL ACTS. THE ONLY DIFFERENCE WAS, I NEVER GOT ANY FURTHER THAN A COUPLE OF PIGGYBACK RIDES. AND WHY? BECAUSE I WAS *TOO NICE A GUY!* I DIDN'T KNOW HOW TO BE DIABOLICALLY MANIPULATIVE LIKE THOSE OTHER GUYS. I FELT TOO *GUILTY* TO DO ANYTHING LIKE THAT. BUT, OH HOW I LUSTED AFTER THE YOUNG PHOEBE IN MY HEART! DID I GET A BLOW JOB OFFA HER? *NOT EVEN ONCE! I GOT NOTHING!* I WENT HOME FILLED WITH SELF-PITY, AS USUAL. (AREN'T MEN HORRIBLE??) I WAS A NICE, DECENT FELLOW WITH A CONSCIENCE, OR SO I LIKED TO THINK. MEANWHILE, THE ARTIST AND PROTAGONIST OF THESE STORIES WAS MANEUVERED, CAJOLED, TRICKED, INTIMIDATED INTO GIVING HER PRISTINE, INNOCENT, GORGEOUS SELF OVER COMPLETELY, AT A TENDER AGE, AS THE STORIES REVEAL, TO A *TOTAL CAD*, AND THEN TO A SUCCESSION OF JERKS, ASSHOLES, CRIMINALS, CREEPS 'N' SLOBS. AND, OH MY GOD, SHE WAS SO BEAUTIFUL! ONE OF THE MOST STRIKING WOMEN I'VE EVER KNOWN (SHE'S STILL BEAUTIFUL — IT'S AMAZING TO LEARN FROM HER COMICS THAT SHE HAD NO IDEA HOW ATTRACTIVE SHE WAS)! I REMEMBER VIVIDLY THE NIGHT I FIRST MET HER AT A CLUB ON POLK STREET IN SAN FRANCISCO. SHE WAS WITH HER MOTHER. THEY'D COME TO HEAR THAT BAND I WAS IN, THE CHEAP SUIT SERENADERS. NOT ONLY WAS SHE PERFECT LOOKING, BUT HER EYES BEAMED OUT AT THE WORLD WITH PENETRATING INTENSITY. HER EYES REVEALED THAT SHE WAS ABOUT READY TO BURST, TO BURN UP. SHE WAS QUIET, BUT SHE WAS A YOUNG FEMALE *DYNAMO*, RADIATING A TYPE OF ENERGY THAT'S DIFFICULT TO LET OUT IN THE WORLD IN ANY "NORMAL" WAY. IT'S NOT AT ALL SURPRISING THAT SHE HAS TURNED OUT TO BE SUCH A POWERFUL ARTIST. I WAS GLAD FOR HER WHEN I SAW THAT SHE WAS DOING THESE AUTOBIOGRAPHICAL COMICS. WHAT BETTER WAY TO CHANNEL THAT *FORCE* THAT'S INSIDE OF HER! PHOEBE IS THE REAL THING; AN ARTIST WHO *MUST* DO HER WORK TO KEEP FROM EXPLODING OR DISINTEGRATING. IT'S OBVIOUS. IT'S ALWAYS RIGHT THERE WHEN YOU LOOK IN HER EYES.

WHEN SHE WAS A FLEDGLING TEEN-AGE CARTOONIST PHOEBE ADMIRED THE COMICS OF ME AND MY MATE, ALINE KOMINSKY. WE WERE SOME KIND OF UNDERGROUND-CARTOONIST-HEROES TO HER. LATER SHE CONFESSED THAT SHE'D HAD DREAMS OF RUNNING AWAY TO *LIVE* WITH US! I'M SAD TO SAY THIS WOULD NOT HAVE BEEN A GOOD IDEA. I WOULD HAVE BEHAVED BADLY. I WOULD NOT HAVE BEEN ABLE TO KEEP MY HANDS OFF HER. IT WOULD'VE BEEN A BAD SCENE ALL AROUND, AND A VERY DISILLUSIONING EXPERIENCE FOR "LITTLE PHOEBE" (WE CALLED HER "LITTLE PHOEBE" BECAUSE HER MOTHER WAS ALSO NAMED PHOEBE). THERE'S ANOTHER THING ABOUT PHOEBE, THOUGH; SHE'S A VERY *TOUGH* WOMAN, PHYSICALLY AND MENTALLY. SHE HAS THIS QUALITY OF BEING INDESTRUCTIBLE. SHE SURVIVED A YOUTH THAT WOULD'VE *KILLED* SOME PEOPLE. SHE CAME OUT OF IT ALL STILL LOOKING FRESH, CLEAR, HEALTHY AND WHOLE. I GUESS SHE HAS EXCEPTIONALLY GOOD GENES. MAYBE SHE HAS A LITTLE PROBLEM WITH LOW SELF-ESTEEM AND LIKE THAT, BUT MOSTLY SHE SEEMS MADE OUT OF HARD RUBBER. SHE BOUNCES BACK... VERY TOUGH. YOU CAN'T HELP BUT STAND IN AMAZEMENT AT A PERSON LIKE THAT.

PLUS, SHE'S AN ACCOMPLISHED, PROFESSIONAL MEDICAL ILLUSTRATOR. IF YOU DON'T THINK THAT TAKES ALOT OF INNER DISCIPLINE, TRY IT SOMETIME! IT'S FROM THIS WORK, I BELIEVE, THAT SHE HAS MOSTLY EARNED A LIVING. HER COMICS ARE SO DENSELY PACKED AND PAINSTAKINGLY DETAILED, IT'S SLOW GOING TO GET A PAGE FINISHED, LET ALONE A WHOLE STORY... NO WAY TO MAKE A LIVING, WHICH IS PARTLY WHY SHE HAS NOT BEEN A TERRIBLY *PROLIFIC* COMIC ARTIST. EVEN SO, I CONSIDER HER STORY, "MINNIE'S 3RD LOVE, OR: NIGHTMARE ON POLK STREET" ONE OF THE COMIC-BOOK MASTERPIECES OF ALL TIME.... RIGHT UP THERE AT THE TOP!

—— FEBRUARY, 1998

P.S. EXCUSE ME, PHOEBE, FOR BLATHERING TO THE WORLD, AND TO YOU, HOW I USED TO LUST AFTER YOU. IT'S THE ONLY WAY I COULD WRITE ABOUT YOUR WORK AND BE TRUTHFUL. I HAVE TO TELL THE TRUTH OR SHUT UP. I CAN'T SEPARATE THINGS. I COULDN'T *LEAVE OUT* MY PERSONAL FEELINGS FOR YOU, EMBARRASSING AS IT MAY BE FOR ALL CONCERNED... OR MAYBE I JUST DON'T WANT TO...

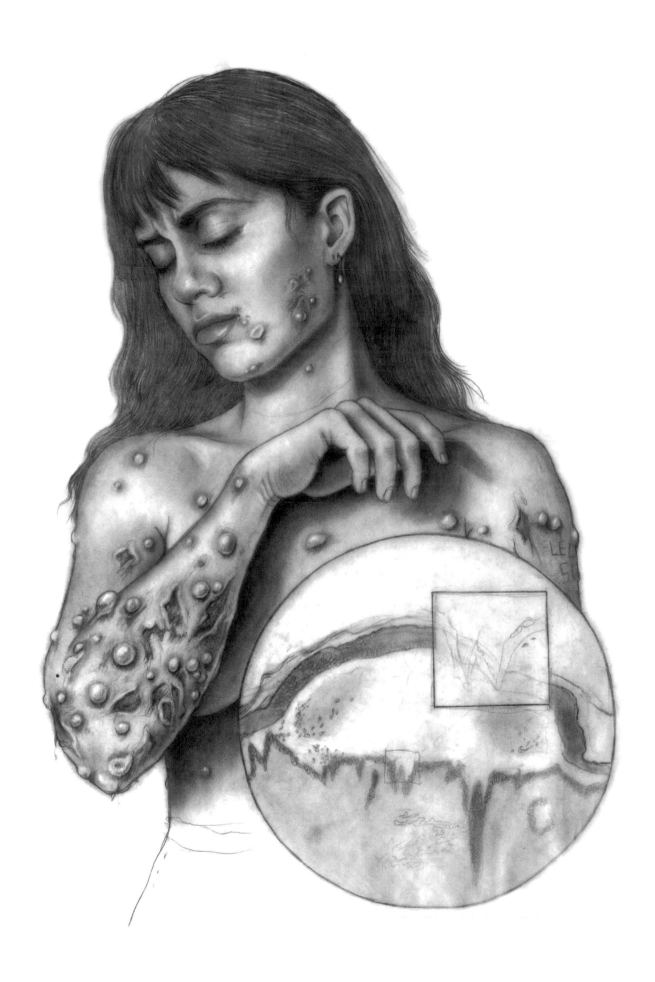

FOREWORD

I NEVER INTENDED THIS BOOK TO BE PUBLISHED. WHEN I FIRST STARTED CARTOONING, AROUND THE AGE OF 15 OR 16, IT WAS AN ENTIRELY SECRET AFFAIR. I'D DRAW IN MY ROOM, PROPPED UP ON MY BED, AND IF ANYONE CAME NEAR, I'D QUICKLY CONCEAL THE COMICS AND PULL OUT A "DUMMY" DRAWING SO NO ONE WOULD KNOW WHAT I WAS UP TO. (I STILL DON'T LIKE ANY ONE KNOWING WHAT I'M DOING.) ONE OF MY EARLY SUCH SURREPTITIOUS WORKS APPEARS ON PAGE 82.

A FEW YEARS LATER, WHEN I DID START GETTING MY STORIES PUBLISHED, I MANAGED TO CONVINCE MYSELF THAT IT WAS OK, THAT I WASN'T TOO MUCH OF A "BAD" PERSON FOR PUBLISHING MY "SHAMEFUL" WORK, BECAUSE, AFTER ALL, HARDLY ANYONE WOULD EVER SEE IT! THE HIPPY DAYS WERE LONG OVER, AND THE "COMIC RENAISSANCE" OF THE MID-EIGHTIES HAD NOT GATHERED MUCH STEAM. IN FACT, "COMIX" WERE CONSIDERED PRETTY EMBARRASSING, UNCOOL STUFF, A NASTY ARTIFACT OF THE "FILTHY HIPPY" ERA. THIS DIDN'T BOTHER ME — AFTER ALL, I'D NEVER BEEN A HIPPY, AND THE MORE REVILED COMICS WERE, THE SAFER I WAS TO DO WORK THAT WAS WHATEVER I WANTED IT TO BE OR WAS ABLE TO MAKE IT. GOOD OR BAD, "PERSONAL" OR NOT, IT DIDN'T MATTER — FEW WOULD EVER SEE IT. (ALTHOUGH, I ADMIT, THE THOUGHT THAT THOSE FEW, BUT NOT TOO MANY, PEOPLE WOULD READ MY WORK WAS A LITTLE BIT EXCITING.)

I DIDN'T HANG OUT WITH CARTOONISTS VERY MUCH. I WAS STUDYING MEDICAL ILLUS-TRATION. MY GRANDMOTHER WAS A DOCTOR AND I USED TO LOVE READING HER MEDICAL BOOKS WHEN I WAS A KID. IT REALLY WAS NATURAL FOR ME TO HAVE AN INTEREST IN MEDICAL ART. MANY OF MY PAINTINGS REFLECT THIS.

IN COLLEGE AND GRADUATE SCHOOL, I WAS SURROUNDED WITH MED STUDENTS AND "FINE ARTISTS," AND FEW OF THEM HAD THE LEAST RESPECT FOR OR INTEREST IN COMICS. IF THEY EVER FOUND OUT I DREW COMICS WHEN I WASN'T STUDYING FOR SOME DREARY NEUROLOGY EXAM OR DISSECTING CADAVERS (I USED TO COME HOME WITH BITS OF FORMALDEHYDE-SOAKED FAT STUCK IN MY HAIR), THEY SAW IT, I THINK, AS A QUIRK WHICH THEY COULD MANAGE TO EXCUSE.

THE WORK IN THIS BOOK SPANS ABOUT 20 YEARS. HOWEVER, I DID THE GREAT BULK OF IT IN THE LAST 5 YEARS. SOMETHING HAS CHANGED IN ME — I NO LONGER FEEL THE GREAT NECESSITY TO HIDE — THIS FEELING HAS BEEN OVERRIDDEN BY MY DESIRE TO DO THE WORK THAT INTERESTS ME. I EVEN HAVE FRIENDS THAT ARE CARTOONISTS NOW. I SUPPOSE THIS CHANGE HAS TAKEN PLACE BECAUSE I'VE PROVEN TO MYSELF THAT I AM ABLE TO FUNCTION SOMEWHAT NORMALLY IN SOCIETY. AFTER SEVERAL ATTEMPTS AT MARRIAGE AND A HISTORY OF FAILURE, TRUANCY, AND EXPULSION IN SCHOOL, I MANAGED TO GET A MASTER'S DEGREE AND ESTABLISH A SECURE FAMILY. WHAT I MEAN IS, I HOPE I HAVE ... I AM WELL AWARE THAT YOU CAN'T BE TOO SURE OF ANYTHING — ALWAYS EXPECT THE WORST, WHILE RETAINING A FAINT (SECRET) HOPE FOR THE BEST, I SAY.

ONE MORE THING— I DIDN'T REALLY EVER HAVE PEMPHIGUS VULGARIS.

—PHOEBE GLOECKNER, OAKLAND, CA, MAY 1998

To A.C. Suits
and
Audrey S.L.M. Gloeckner-
Kalousek

♡

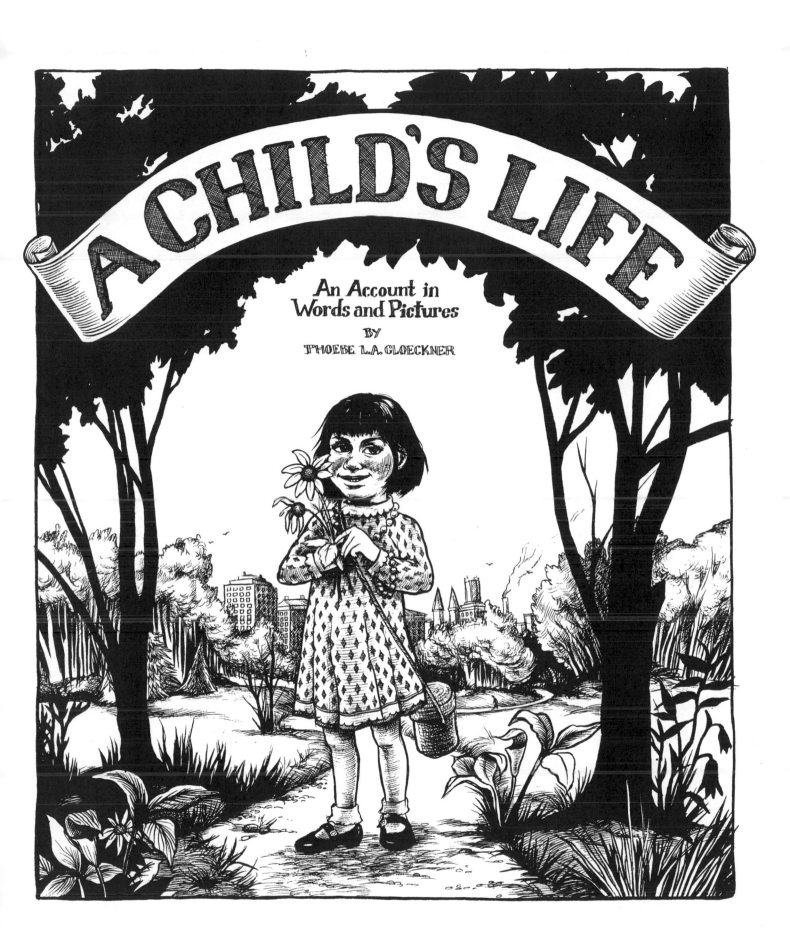

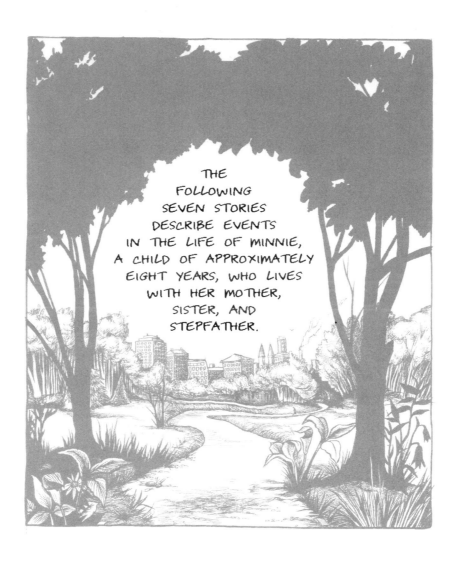

THE
FOLLOWING
SEVEN STORIES
DESCRIBE EVENTS
IN THE LIFE OF MINNIE,
A CHILD OF APPROXIMATELY
EIGHT YEARS, WHO LIVES
WITH HER MOTHER,
SISTER, AND
STEPFATHER.

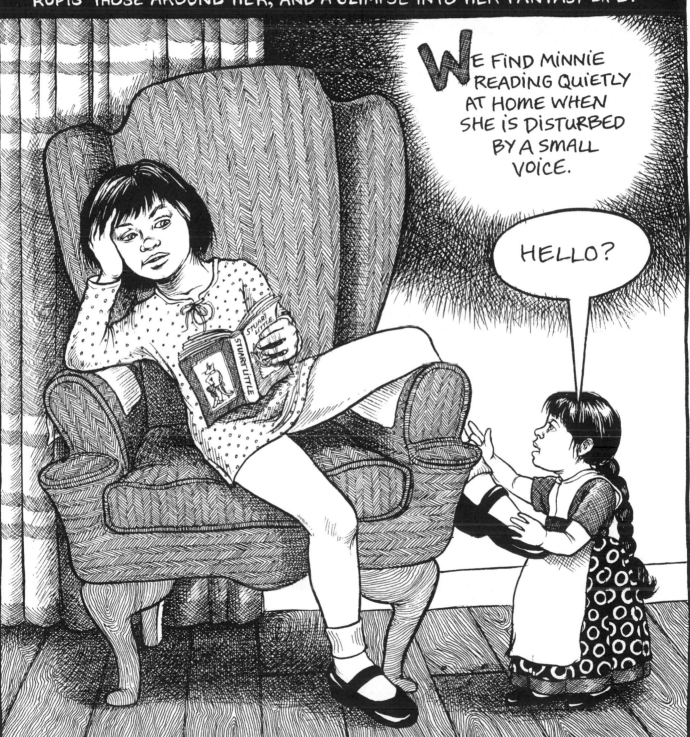

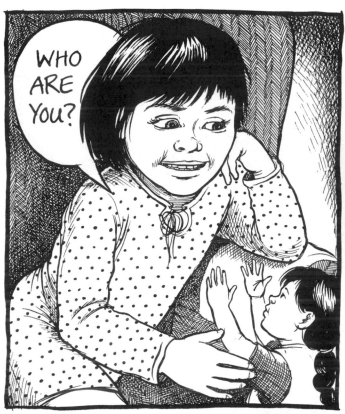

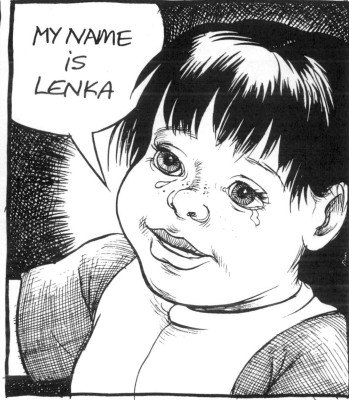

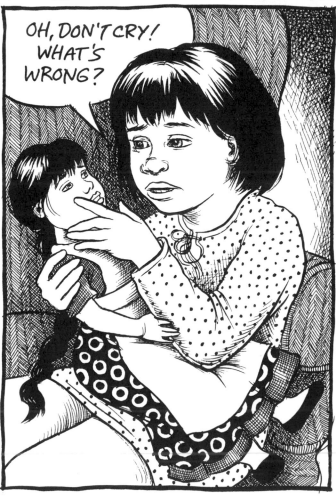

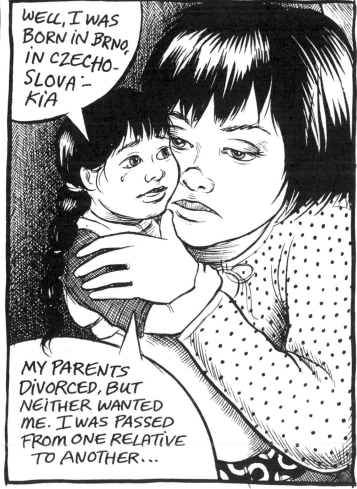

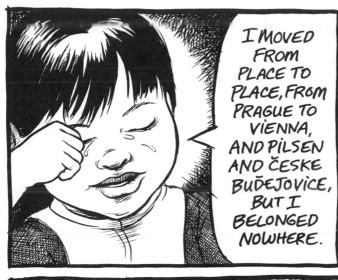

I MOVED FROM PLACE TO PLACE, FROM PRAGUE TO VIENNA, AND PILSEN AND ČESKE BUDĚJOVICE, BUT I BELONGED NOWHERE.

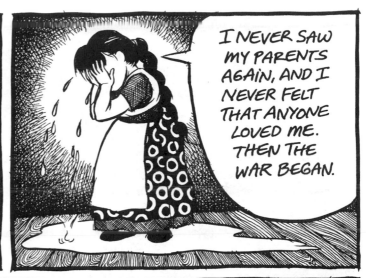

I NEVER SAW MY PARENTS AGAIN, AND I NEVER FELT THAT ANYONE LOVED ME. THEN THE WAR BEGAN.

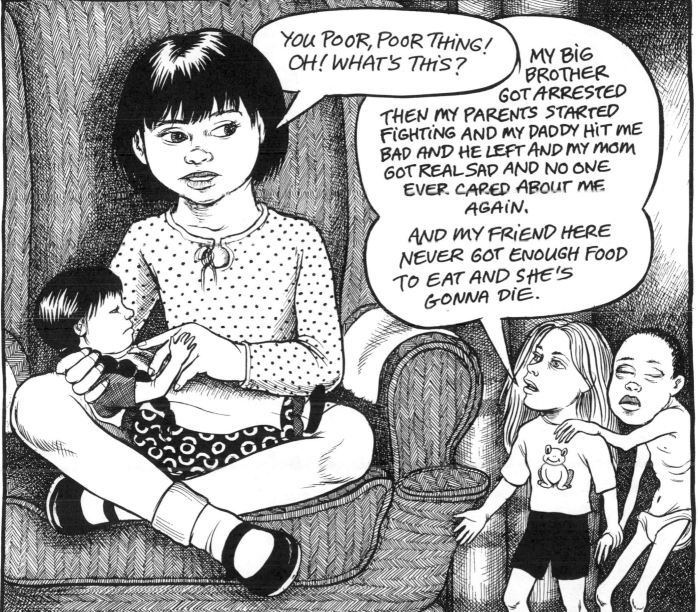

YOU POOR, POOR THING! OH! WHAT'S THIS?

MY BIG BROTHER GOT ARRESTED THEN MY PARENTS STARTED FIGHTING AND MY DADDY HIT ME BAD AND HE LEFT AND MY MOM GOT REAL SAD AND NO ONE EVER CARED ABOUT ME AGAIN.

AND MY FRIEND HERE NEVER GOT ENOUGH FOOD TO EAT AND SHE'S GONNA DIE.

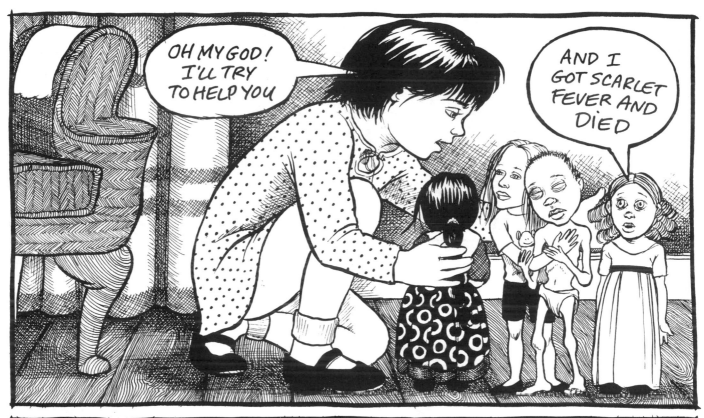

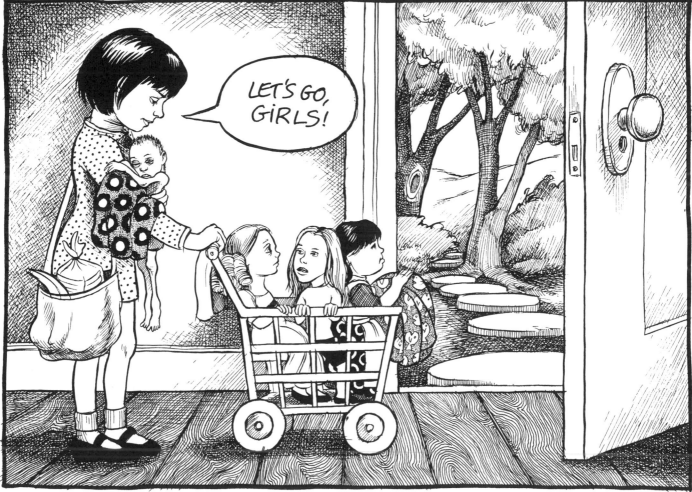

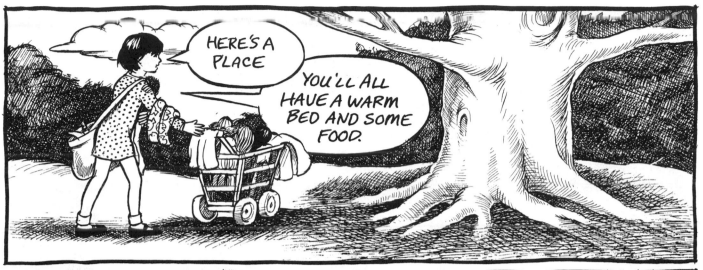

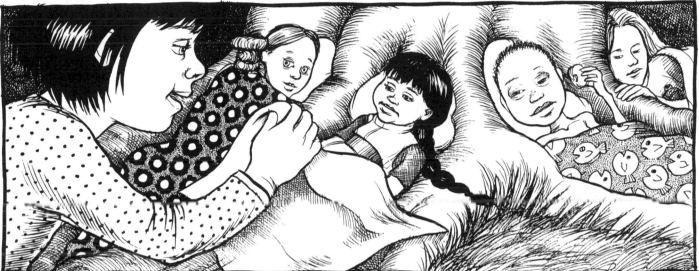

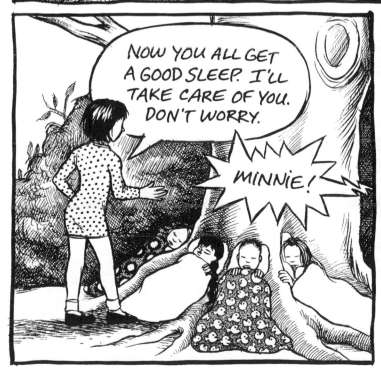

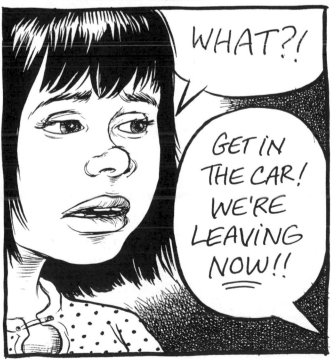

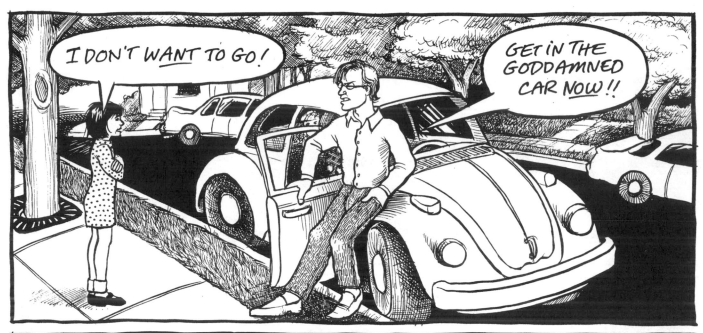

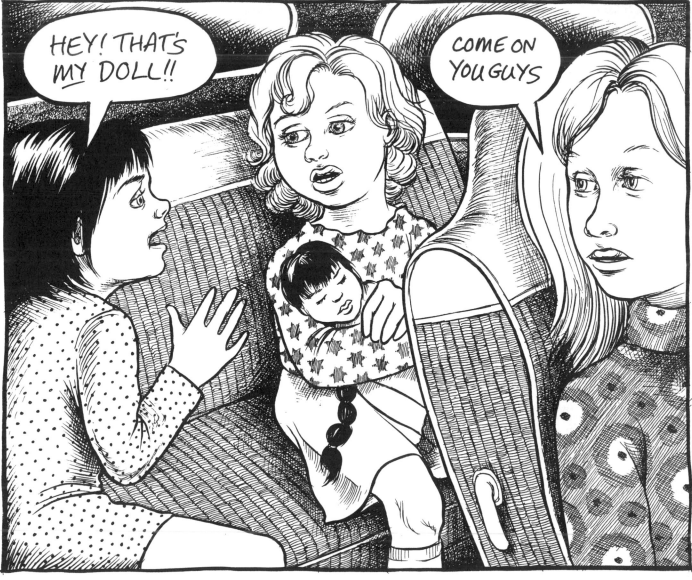

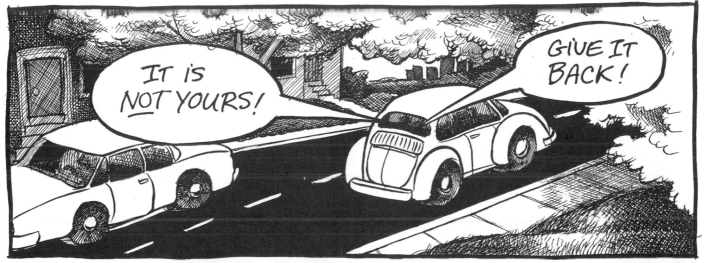

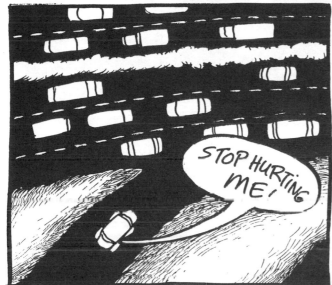

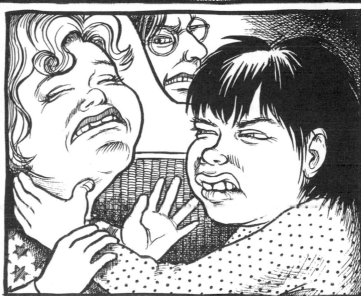

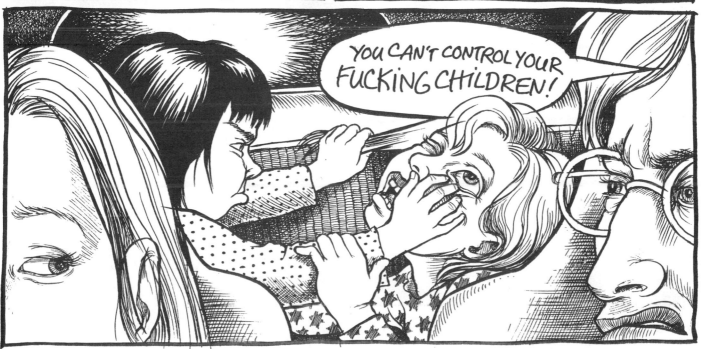

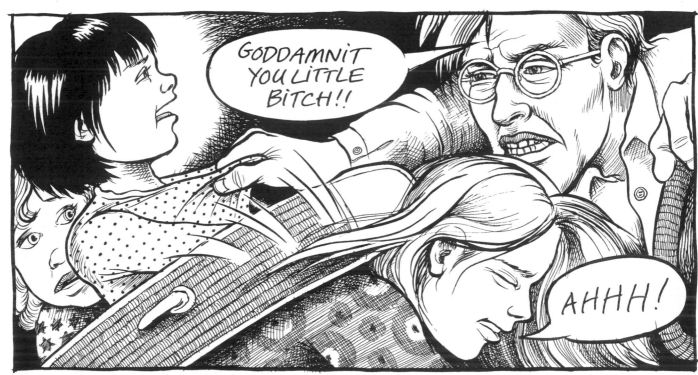

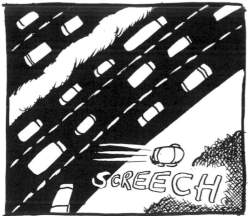

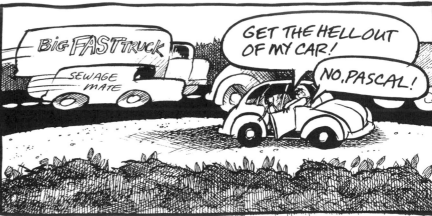

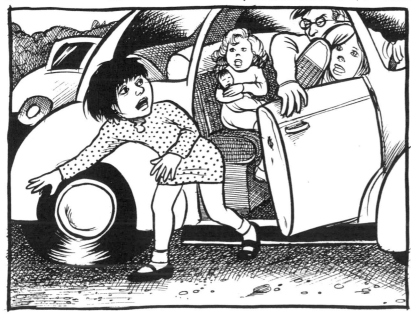

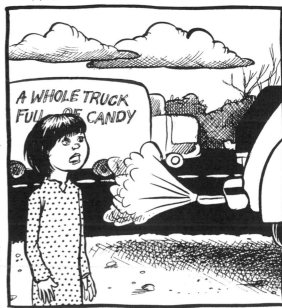

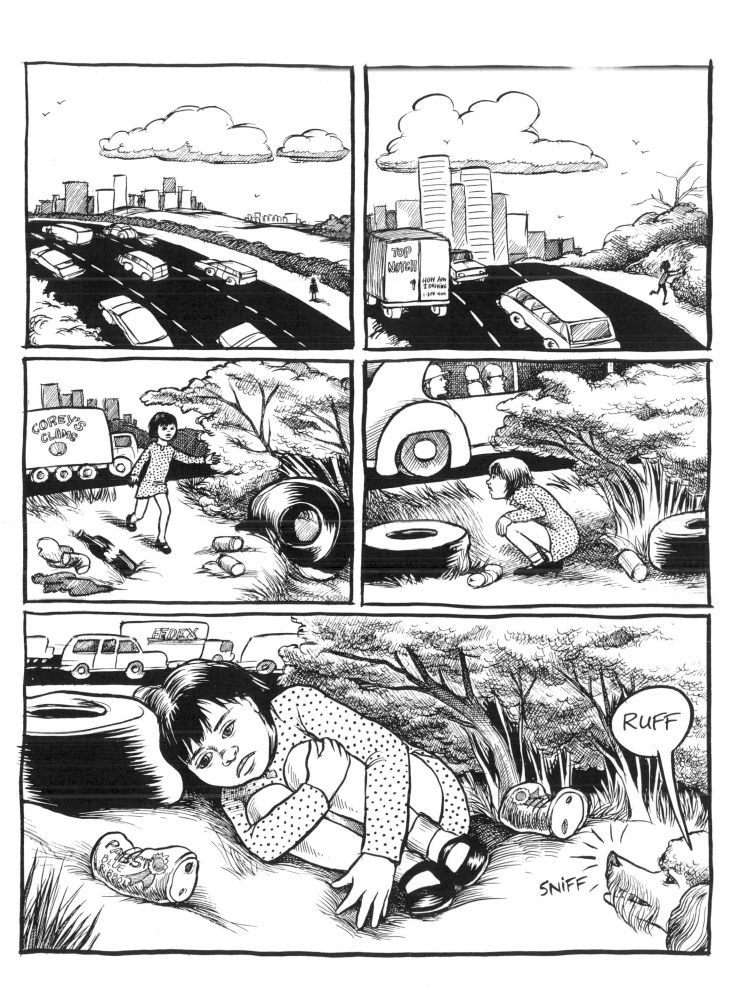

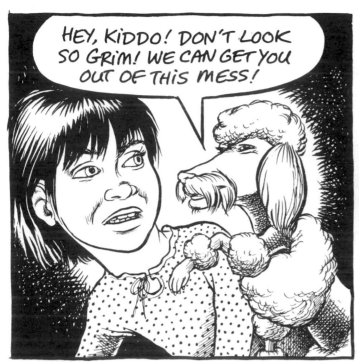

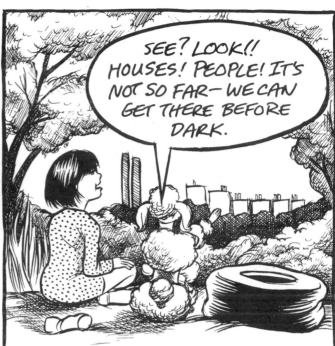

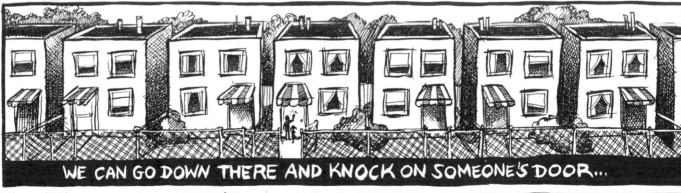

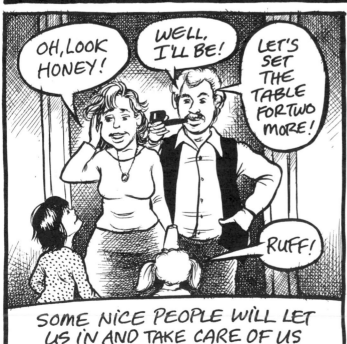

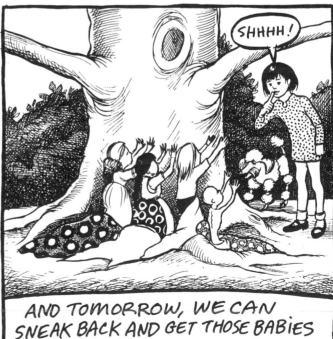

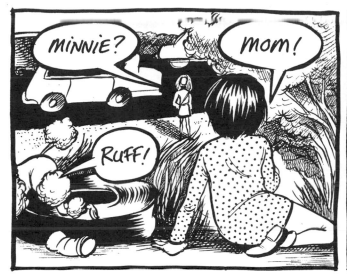

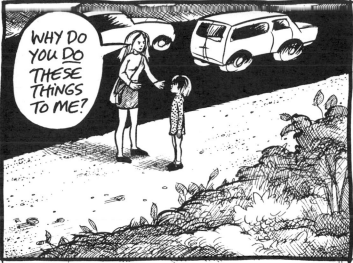

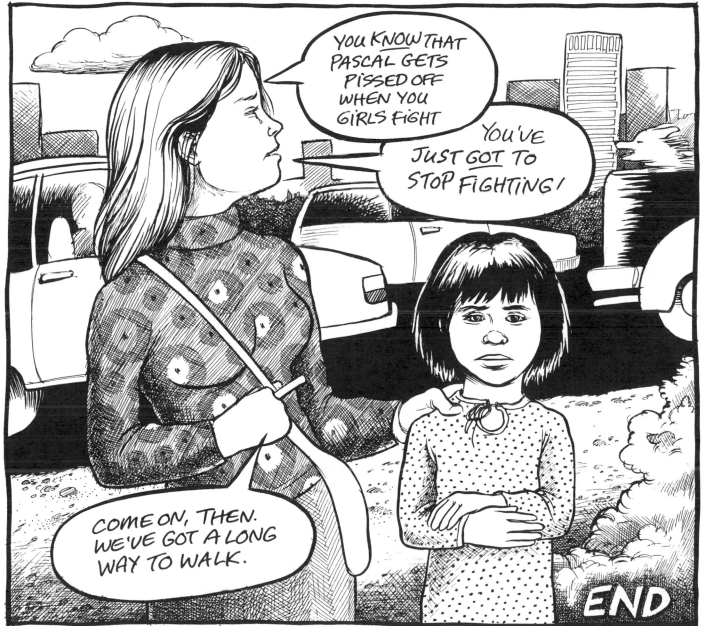

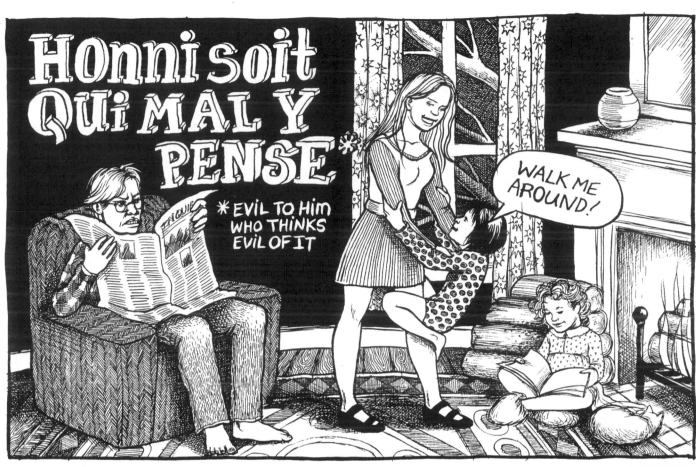

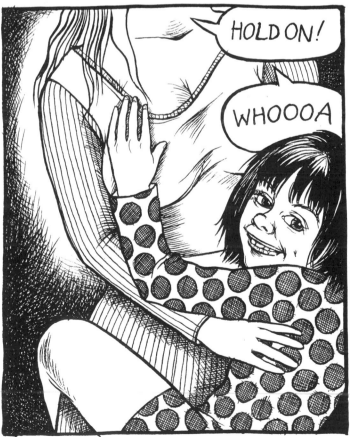

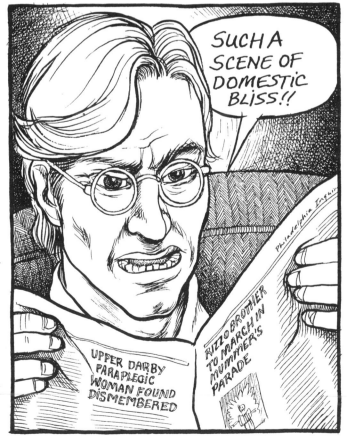

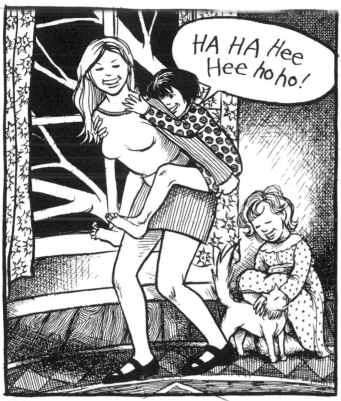

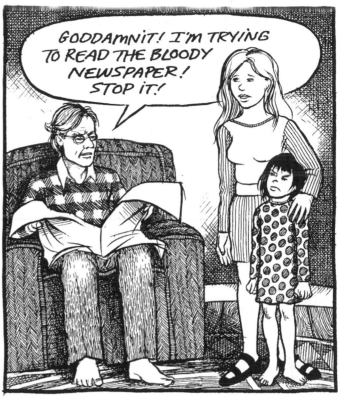

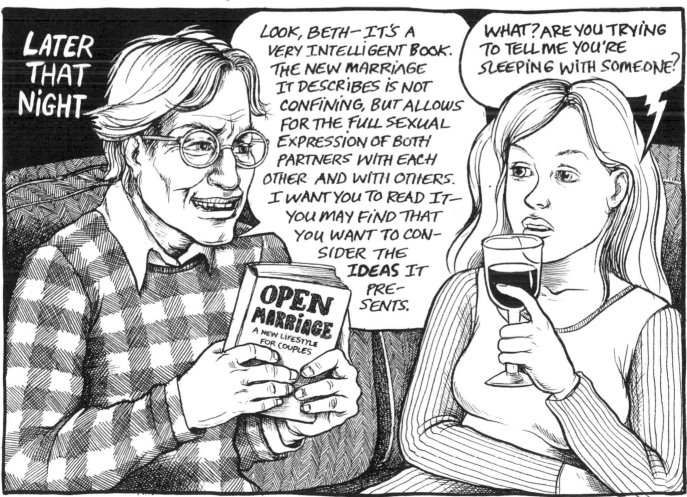

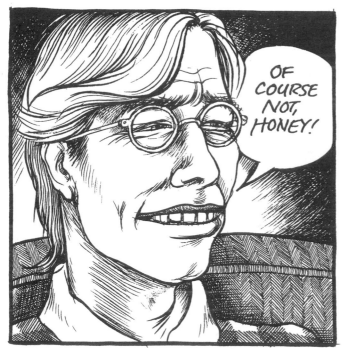

OF COURSE NOT, HONEY!

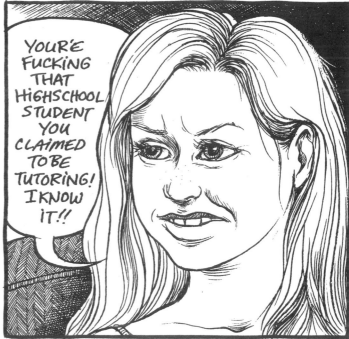

YOU'RE FUCKING THAT HIGHSCHOOL STUDENT YOU CLAIMED TO BE TUTORING! I KNOW IT!!

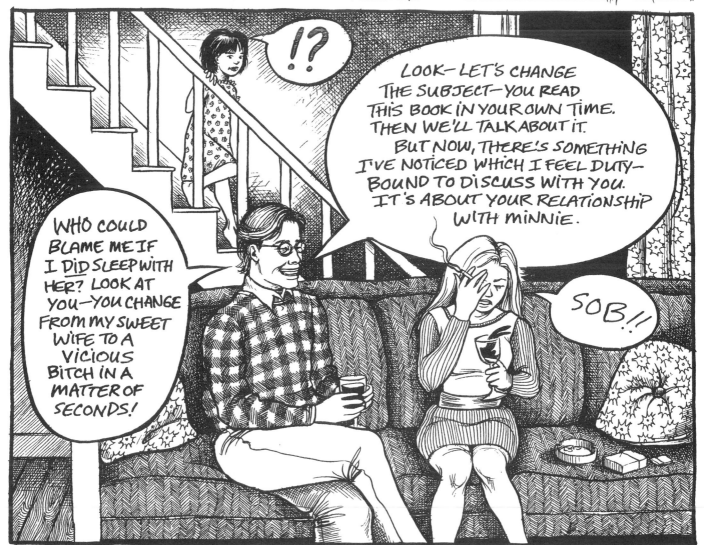

!?

LOOK— LET'S CHANGE THE SUBJECT— YOU READ THIS BOOK IN YOUR OWN TIME. THEN WE'LL TALK ABOUT IT.
BUT NOW, THERE'S SOMETHING I'VE NOTICED WHICH I FEEL DUTY-BOUND TO DISCUSS WITH YOU. IT'S ABOUT YOUR RELATIONSHIP WITH MINNIE.

WHO COULD BLAME ME IF I DID SLEEP WITH HER? LOOK AT YOU— YOU CHANGE FROM MY SWEET WIFE TO A VICIOUS BITCH IN A MATTER OF SECONDS!

SOB!!

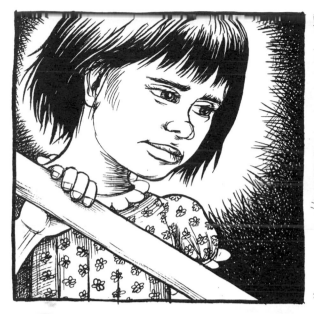

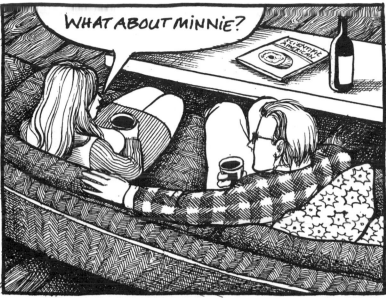

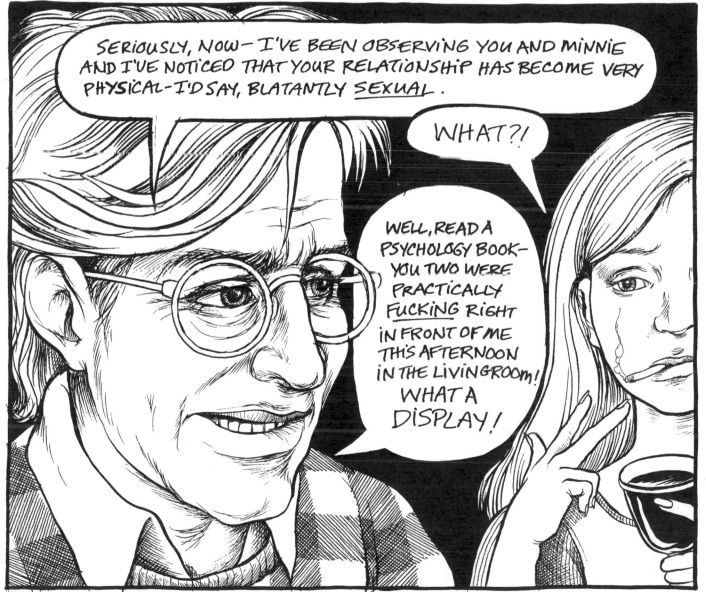

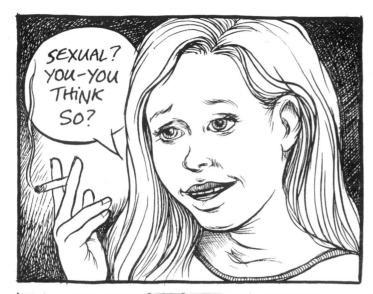
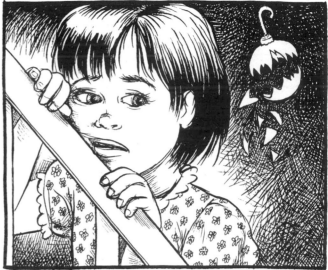
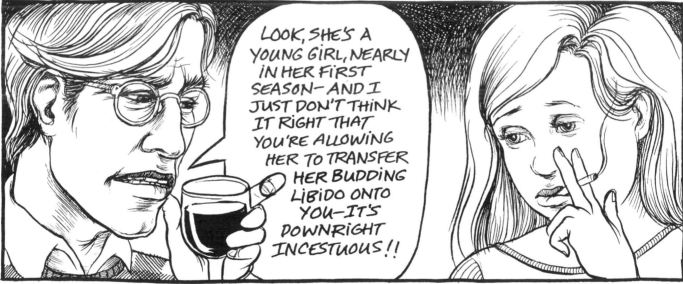
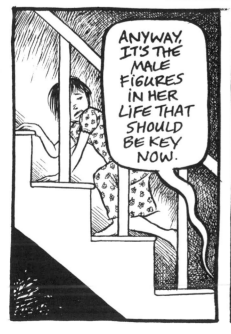
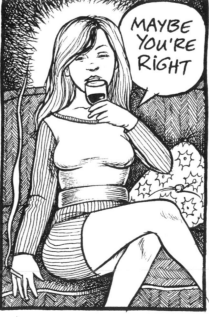
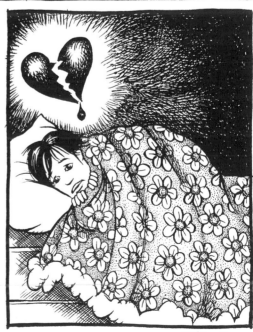

FIN.

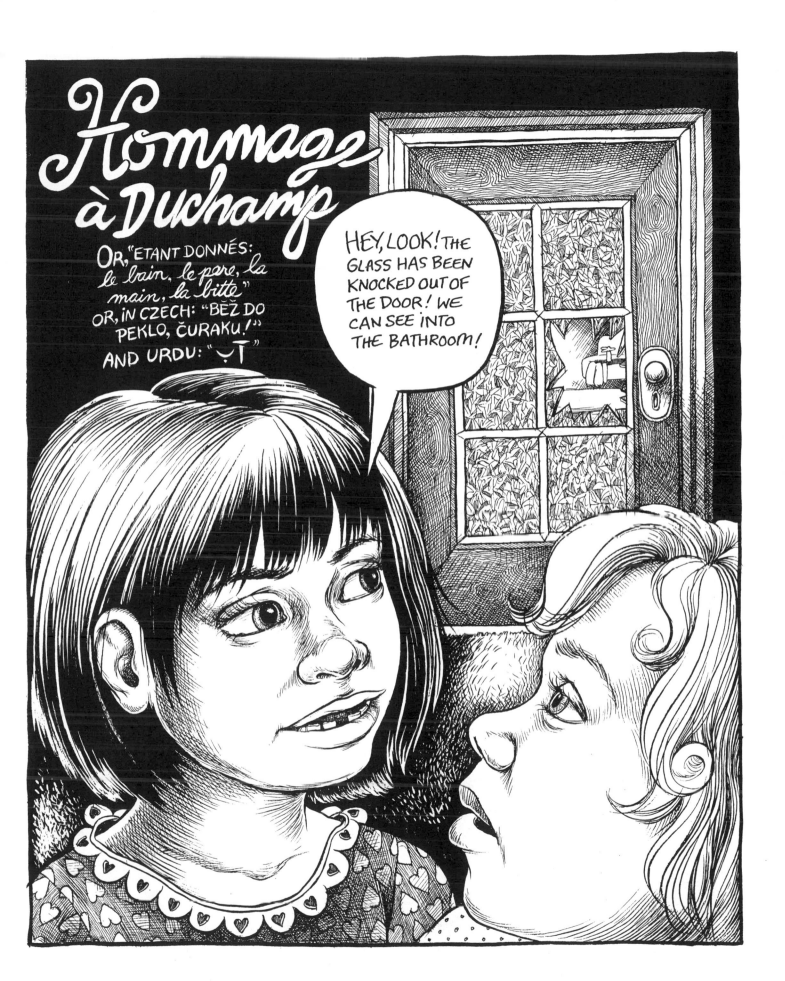

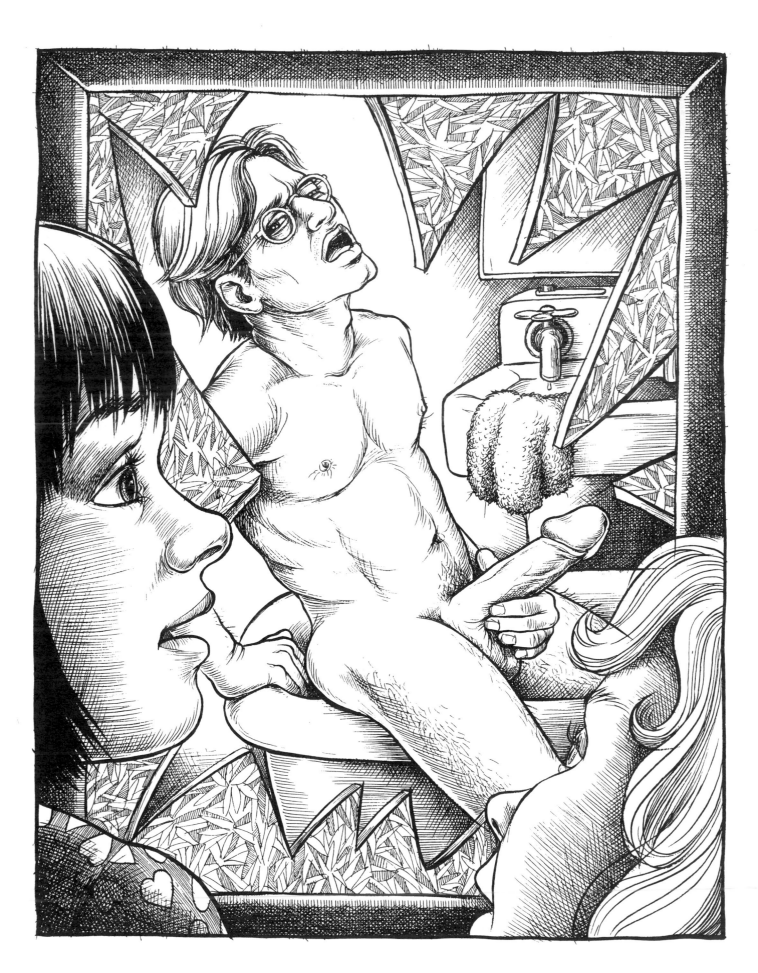

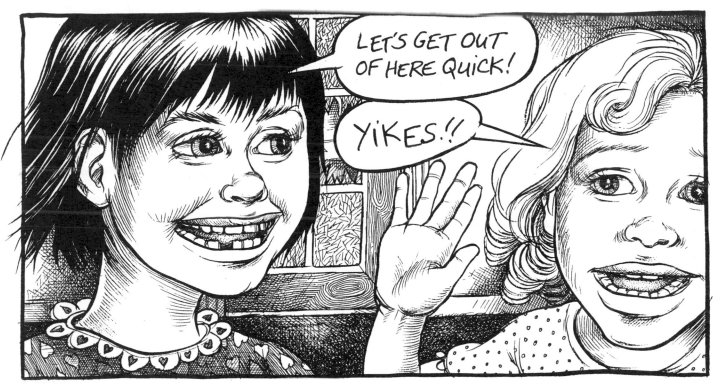

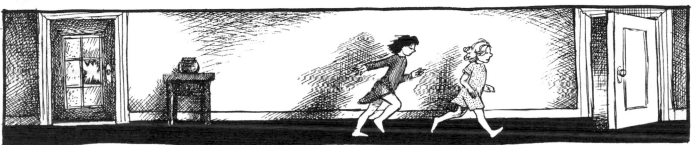

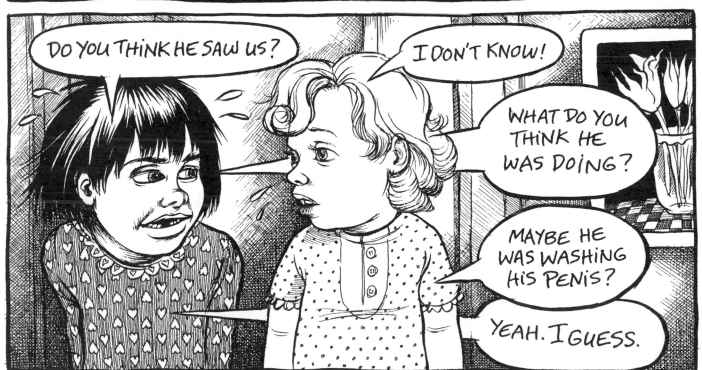

ENDO

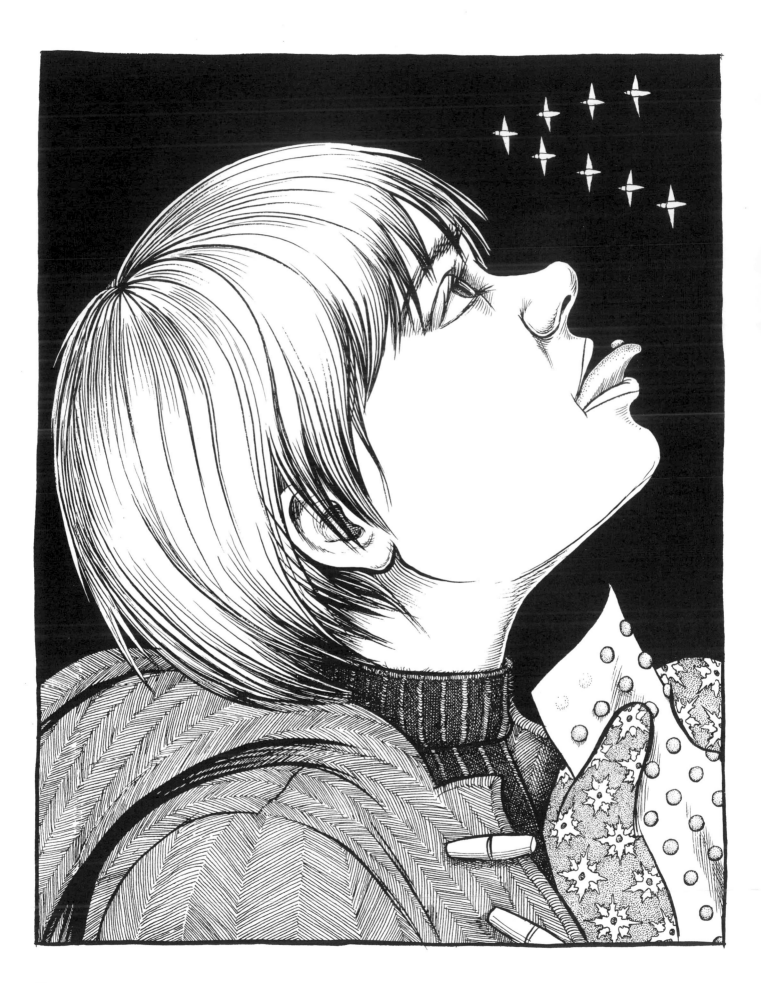

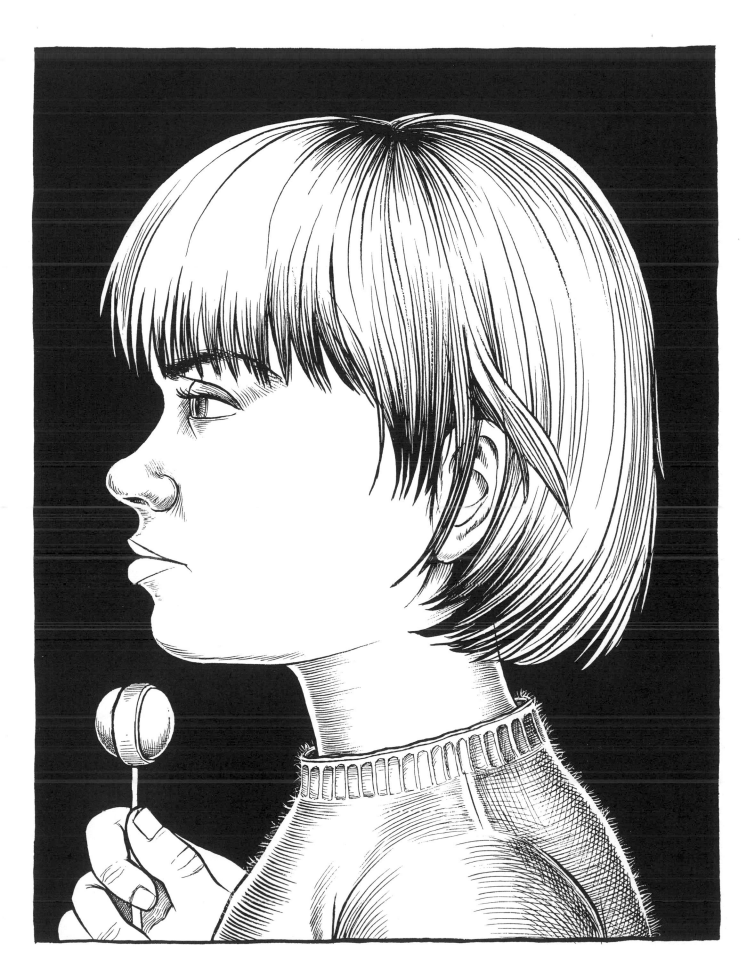

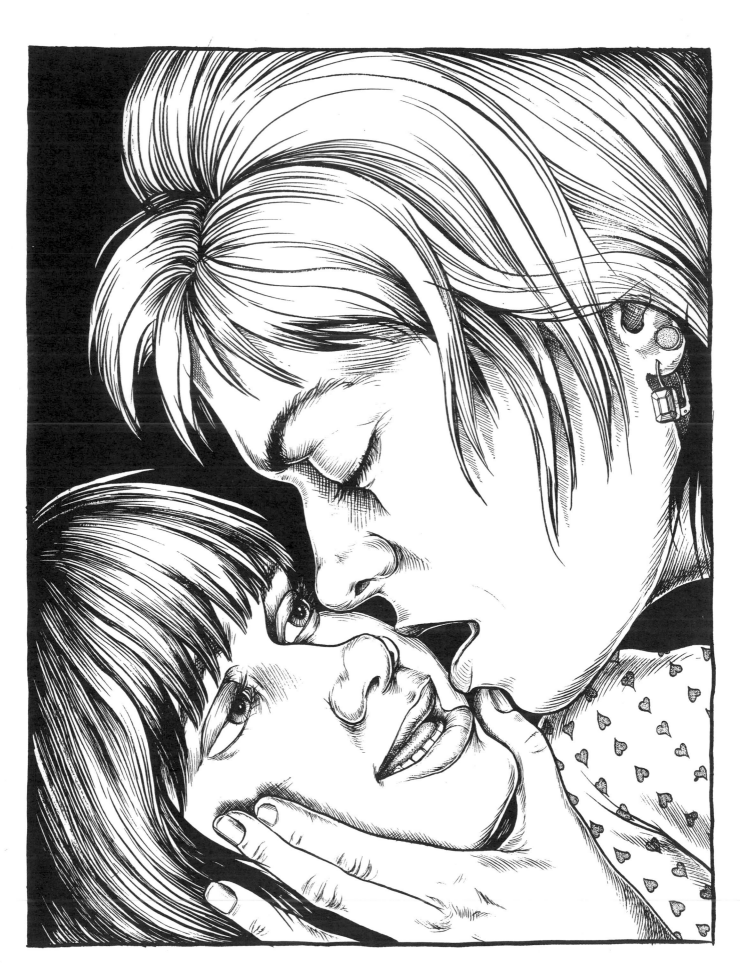

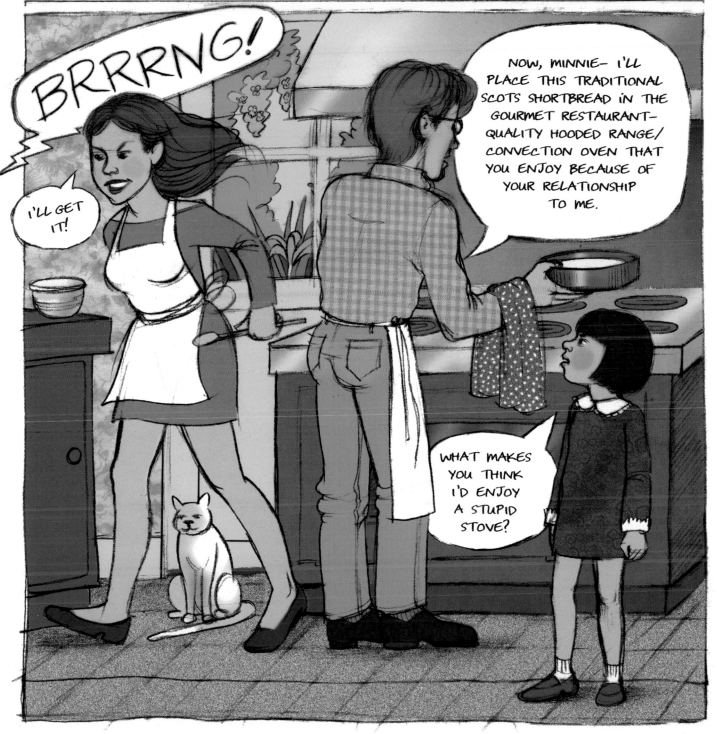

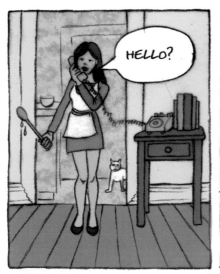

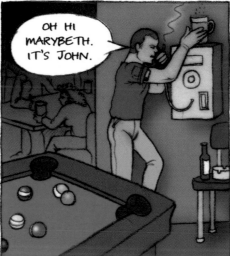

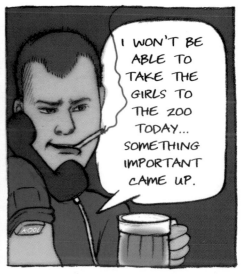

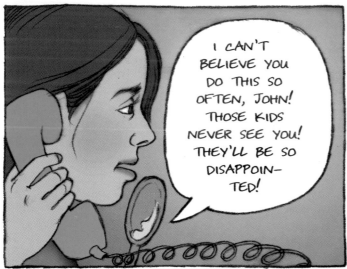

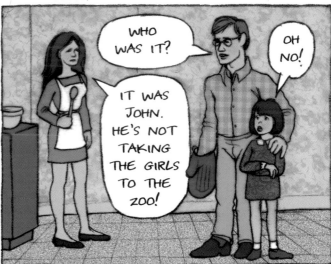

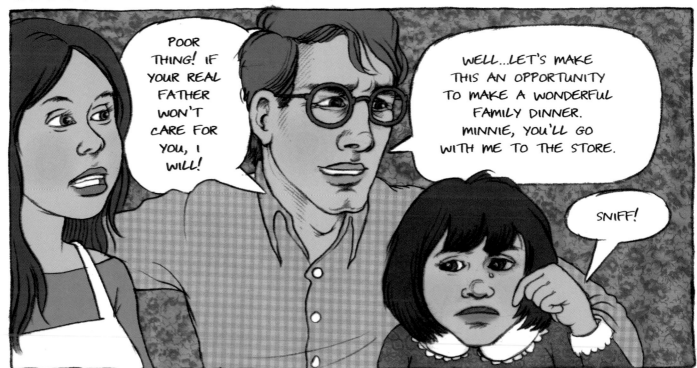

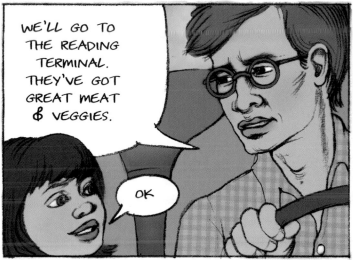

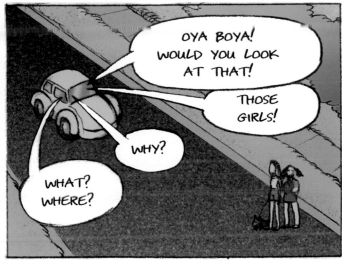

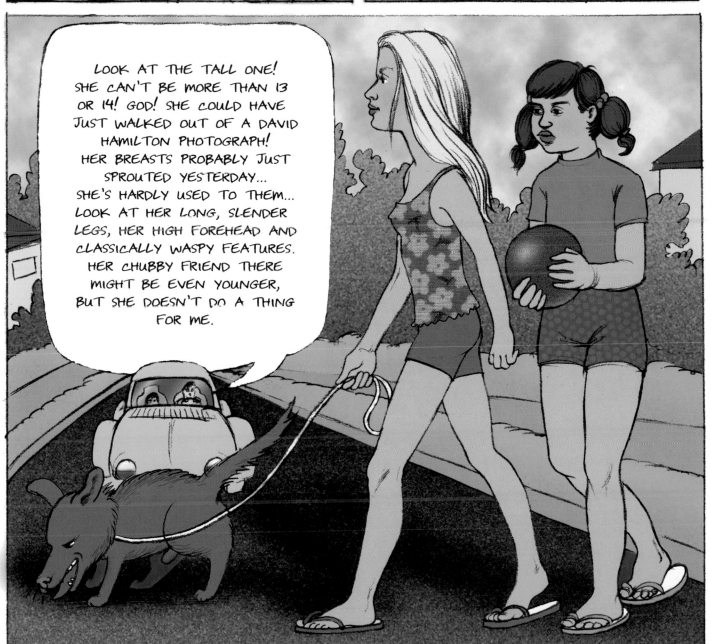

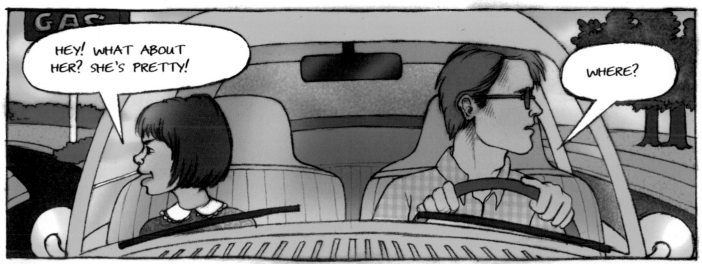

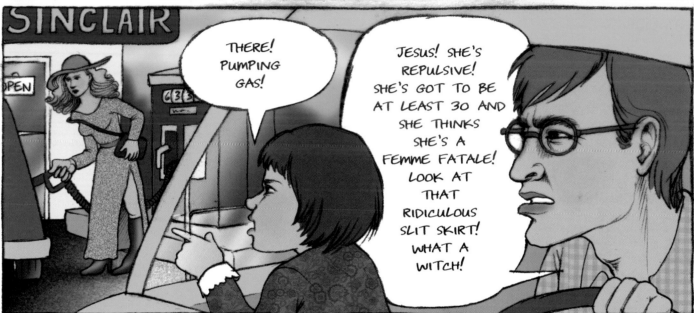

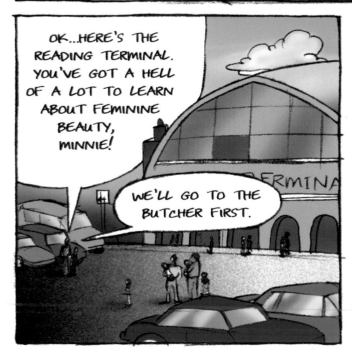

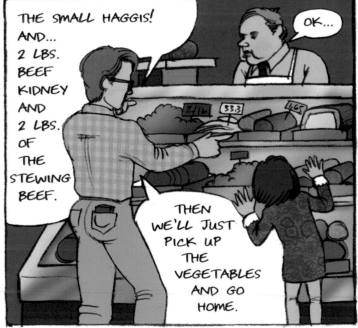

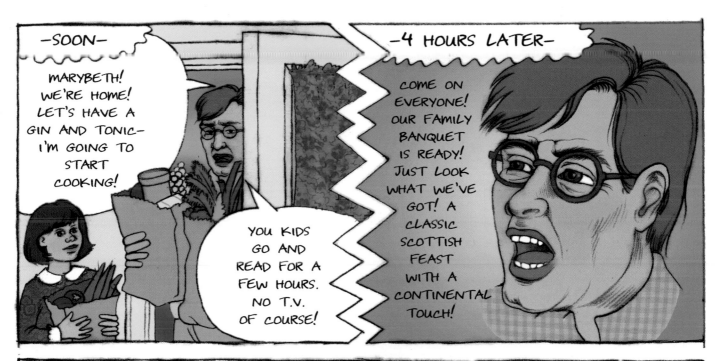

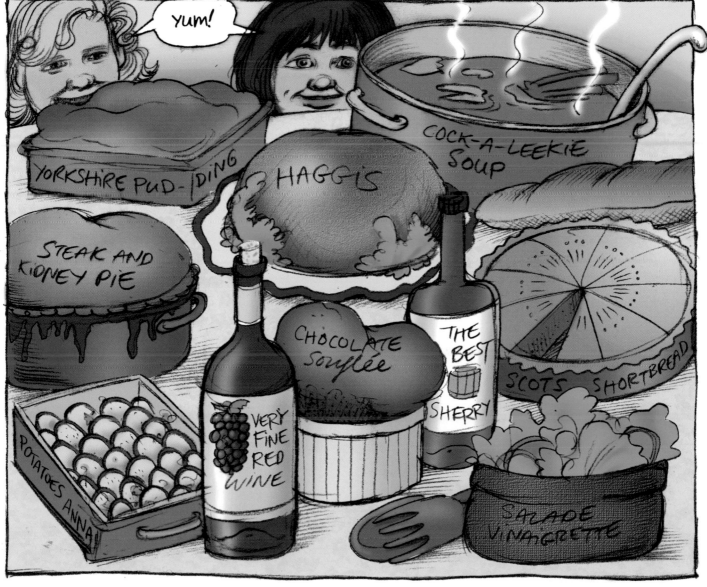

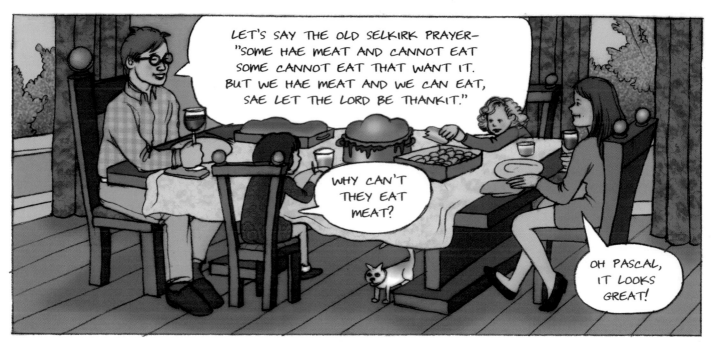

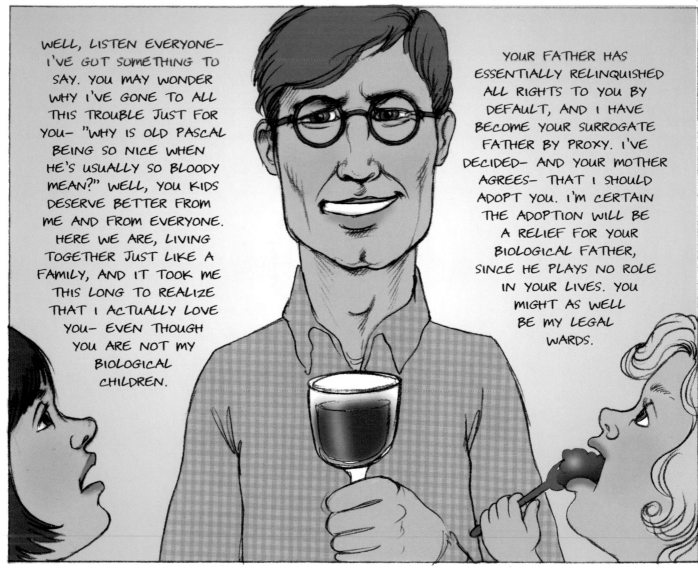

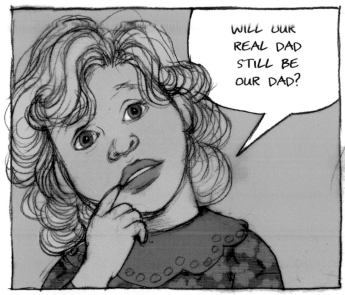

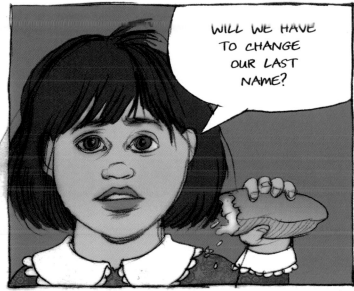

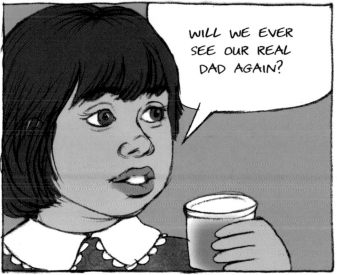

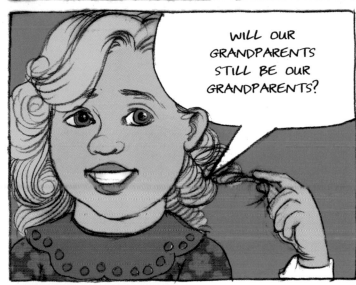

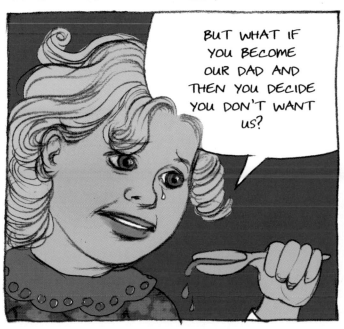

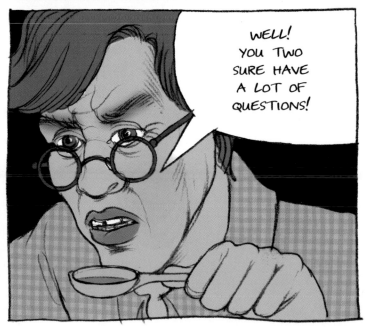

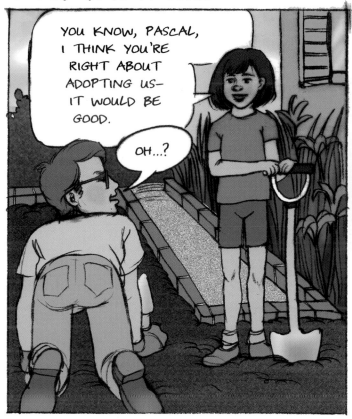

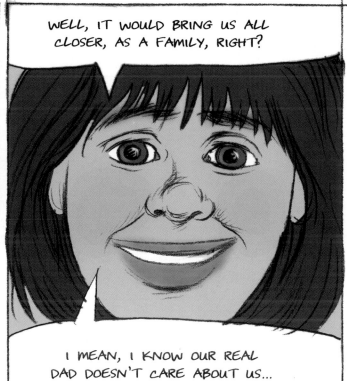

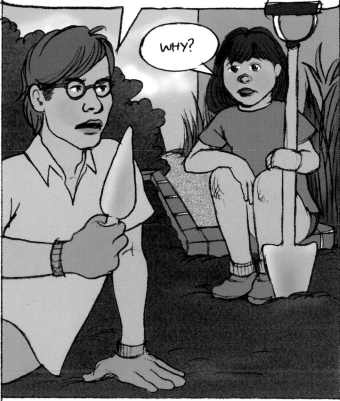

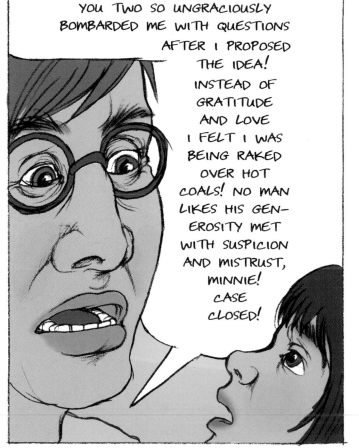

THE END.

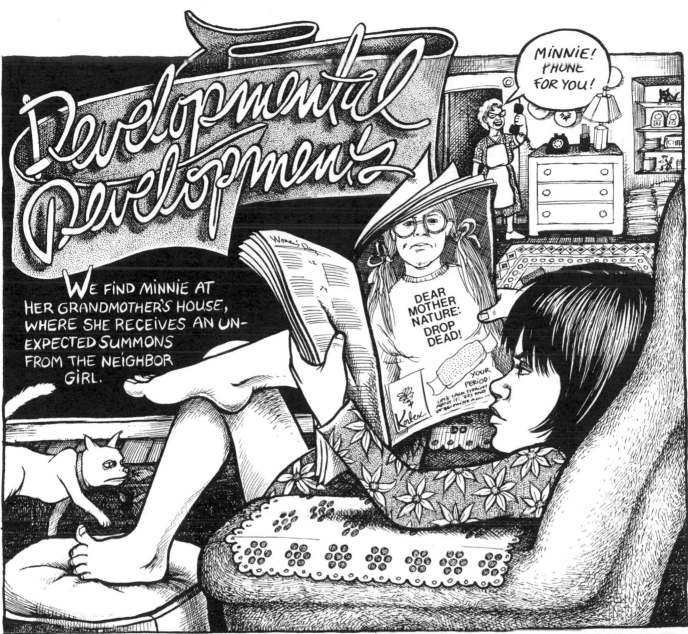

Developmental Developments

WE FIND MINNIE AT HER GRANDMOTHER'S HOUSE, WHERE SHE RECEIVES AN UNEXPECTED SUMMONS FROM THE NEIGHBOR GIRL.

MINNIE! PHONE FOR YOU!

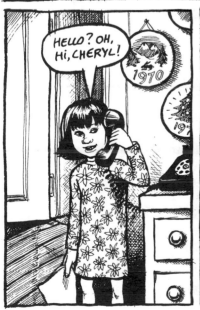

HELLO? OH, HI, CHERYL!

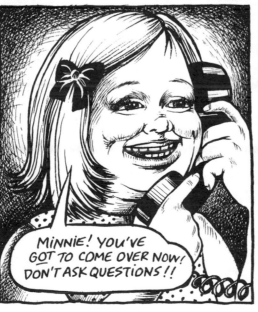

MINNIE! YOU'VE GOT TO COME OVER NOW! DON'T ASK QUESTIONS!!

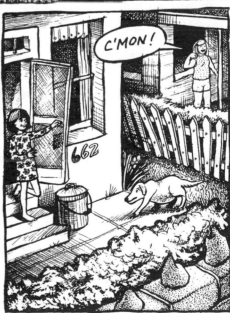

C'MON!

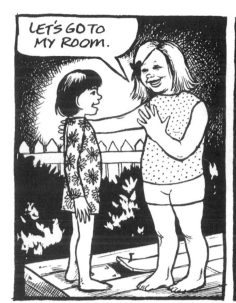

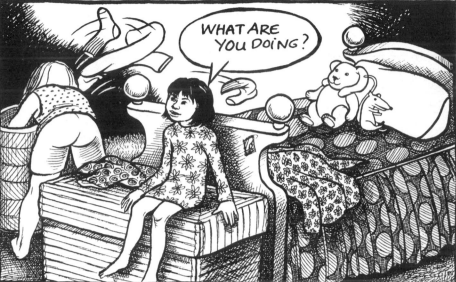

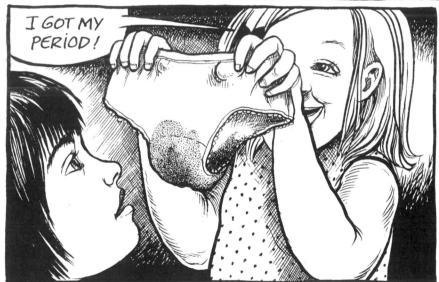

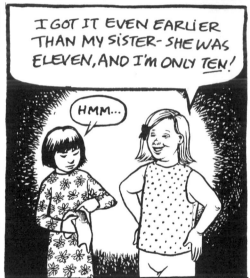

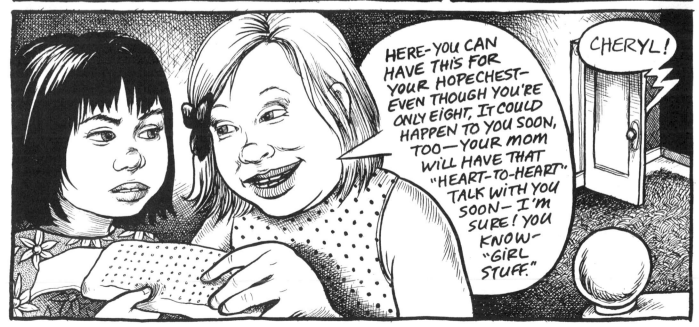

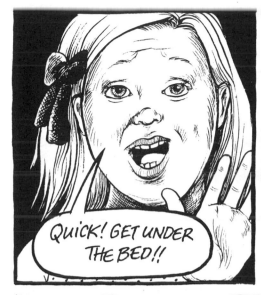

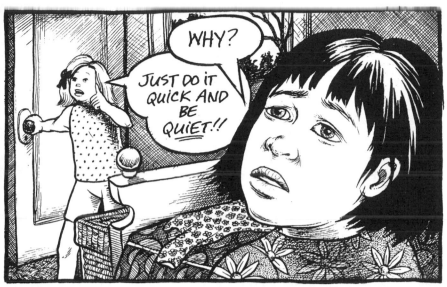

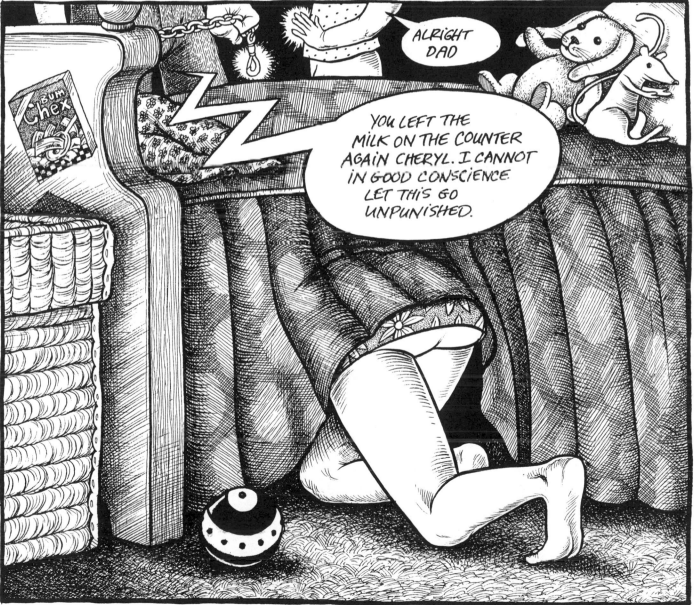

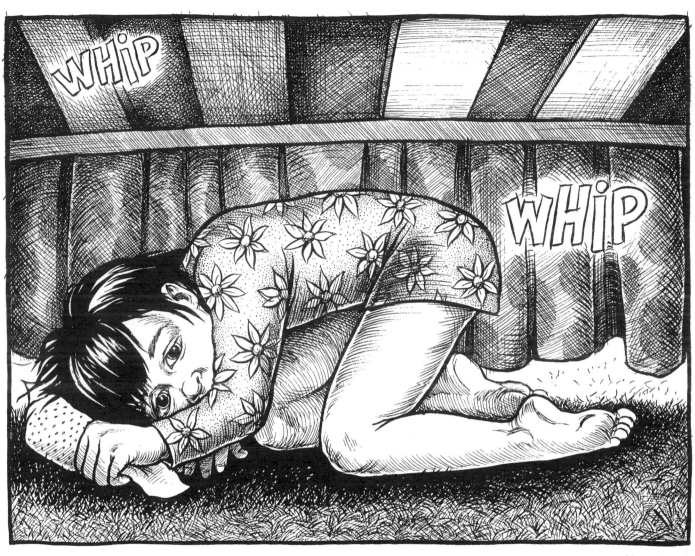

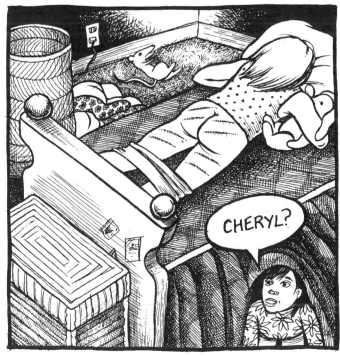

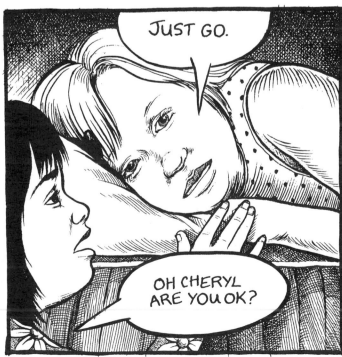

SO, MINNIE WENT BACK TO GRANNY'S....

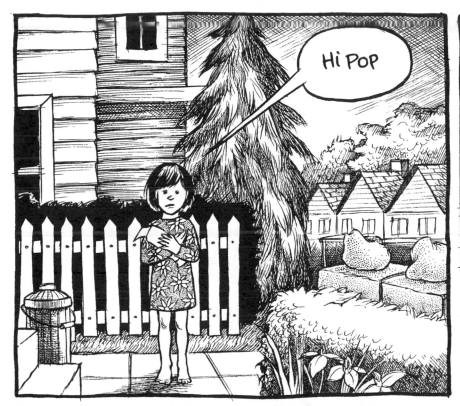
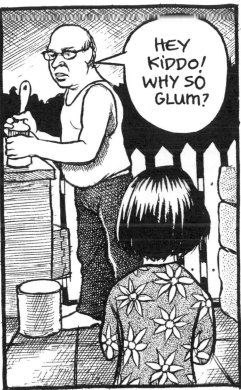
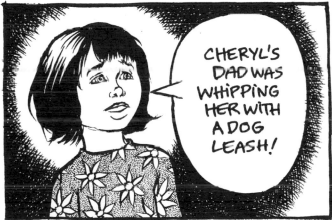
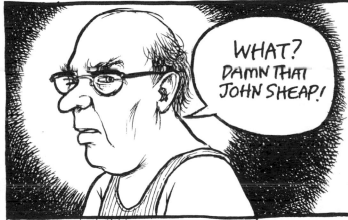
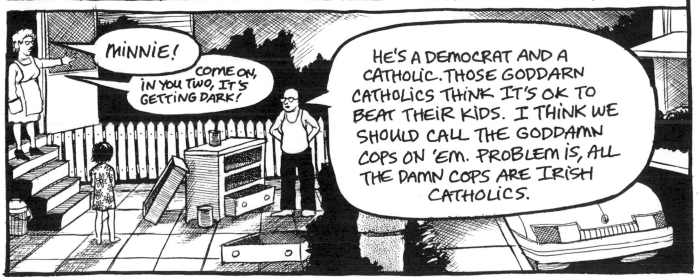

That night...

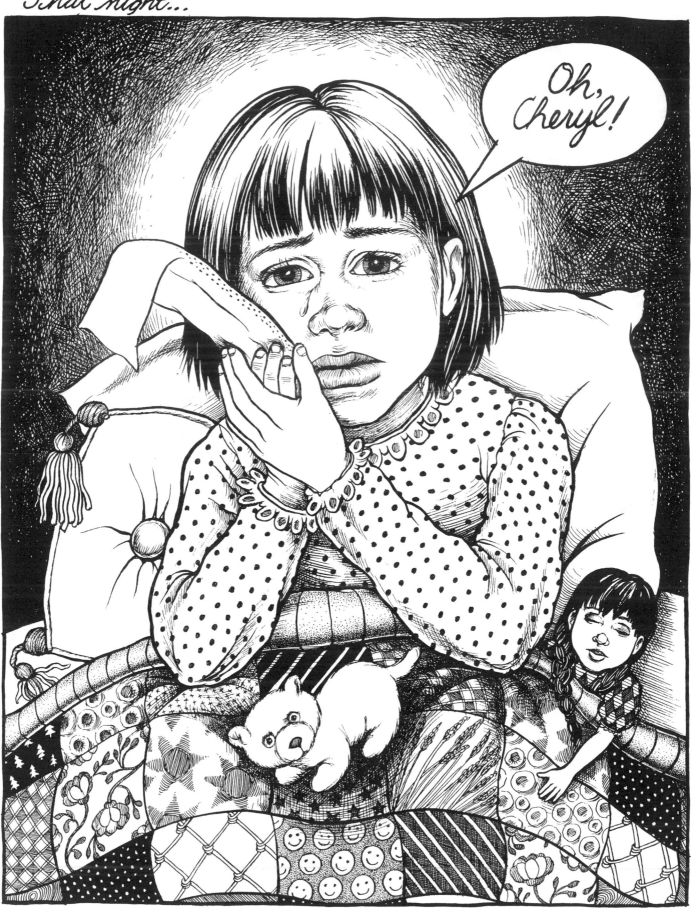

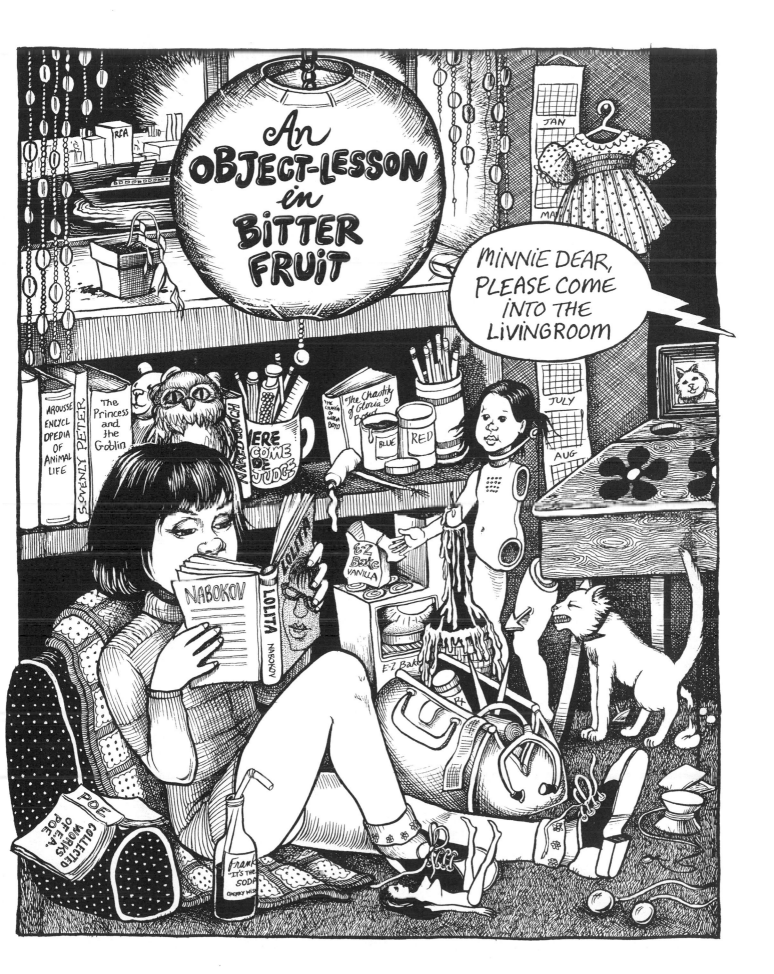

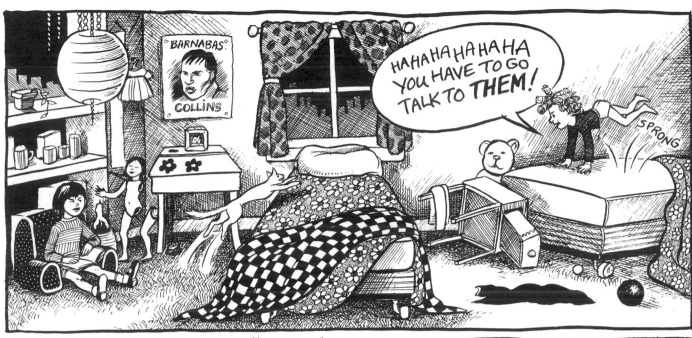

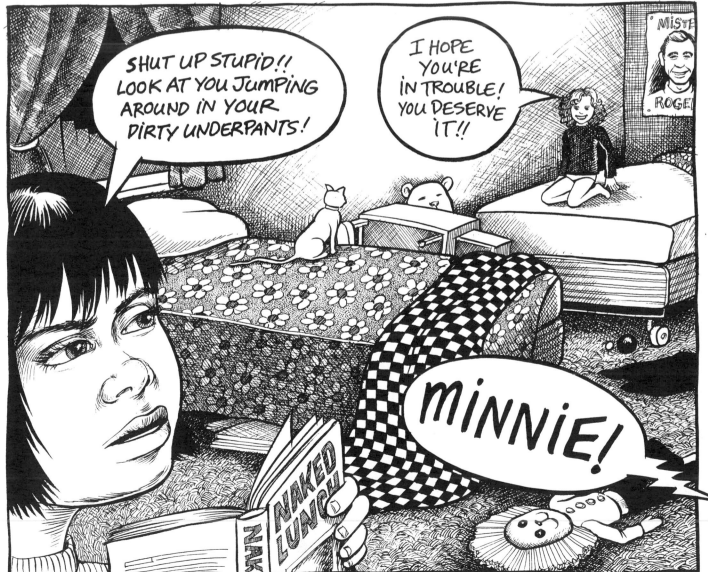

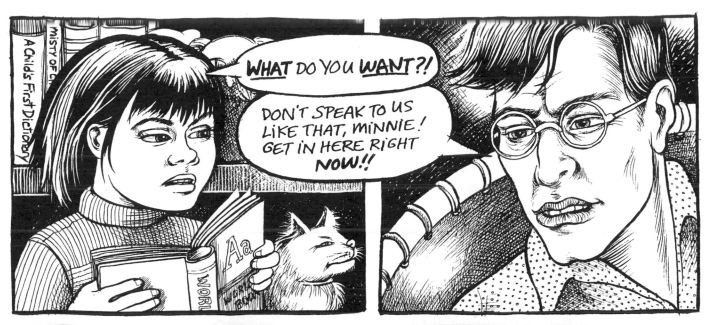

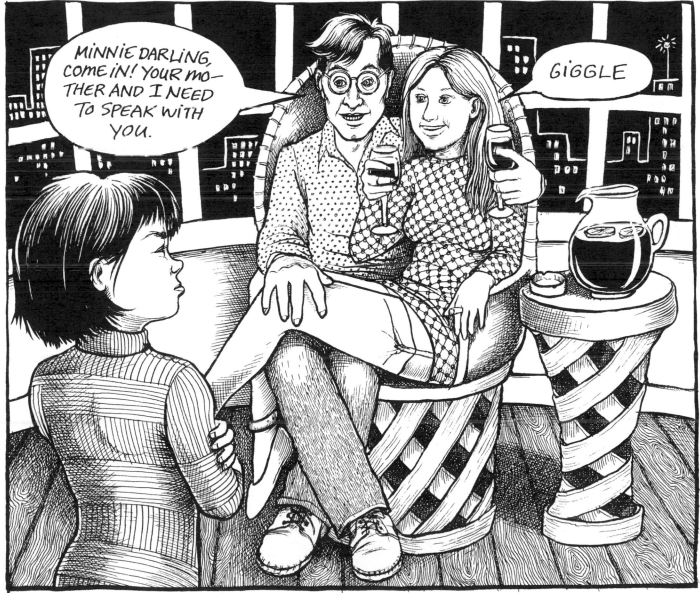

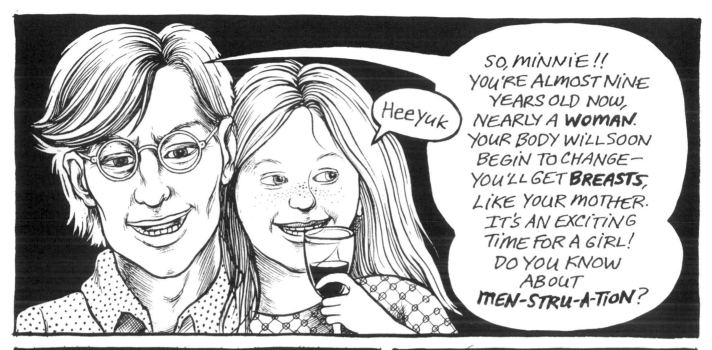

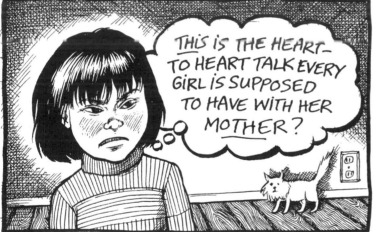

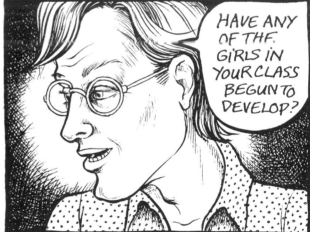

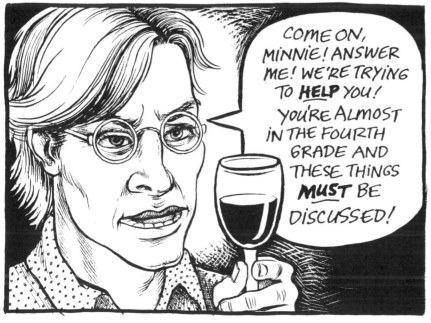

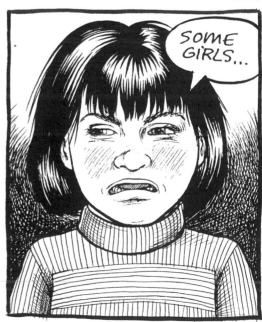

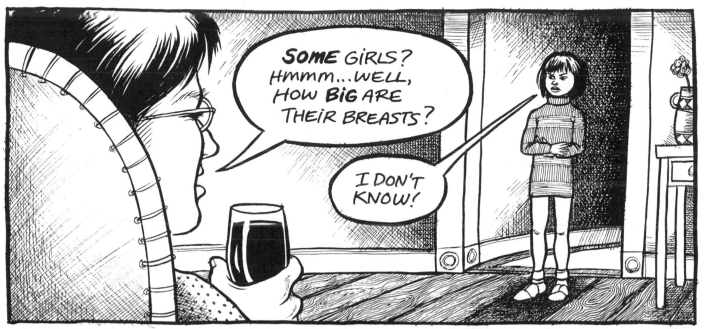

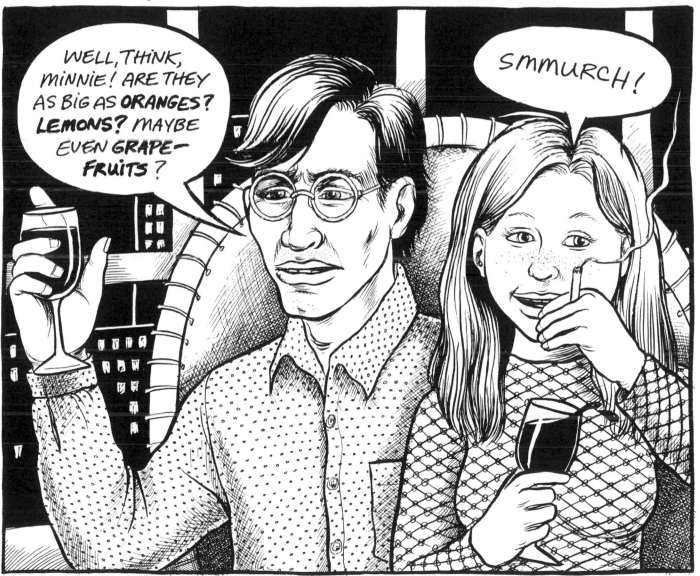

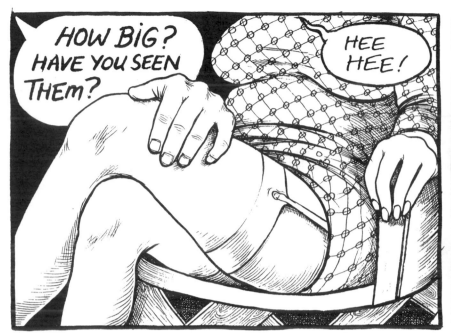

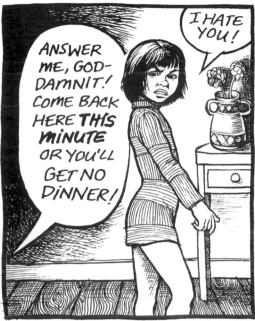

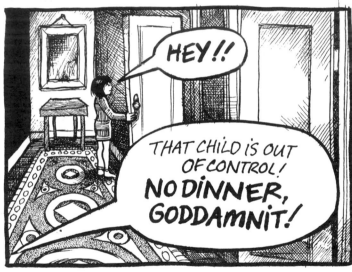

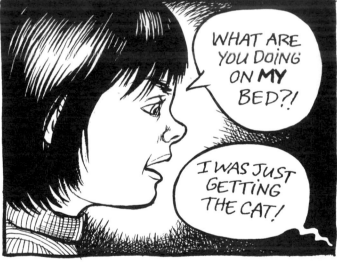

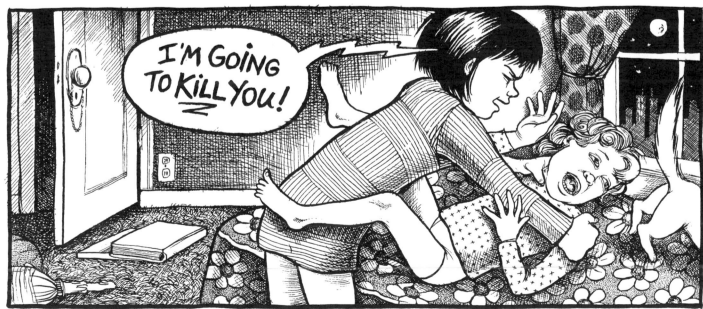

THE END

STEPFATHERLY COUNSEL

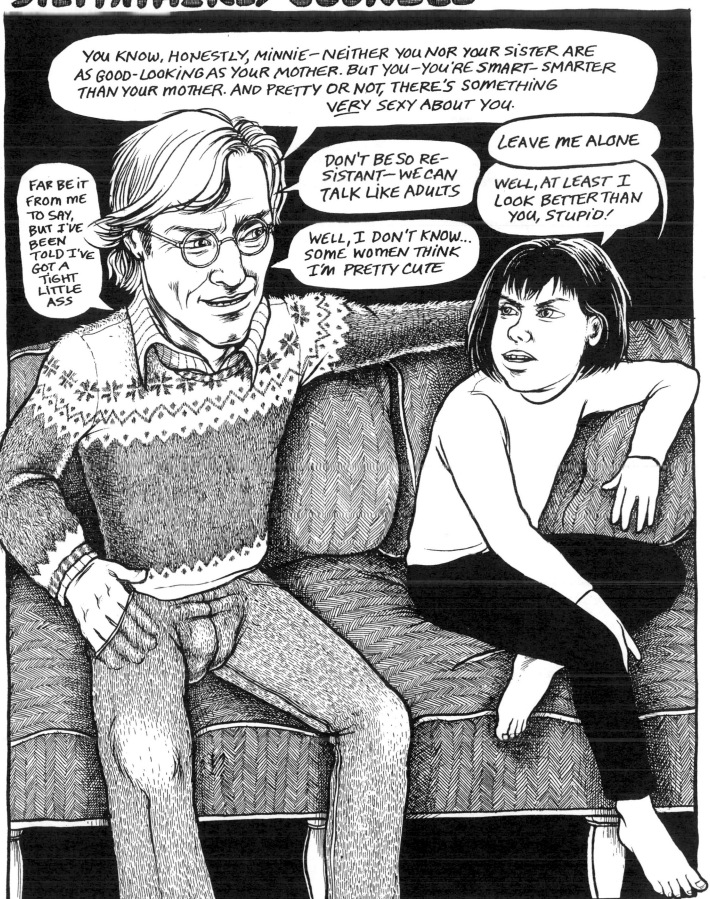

ABSOLUTE END

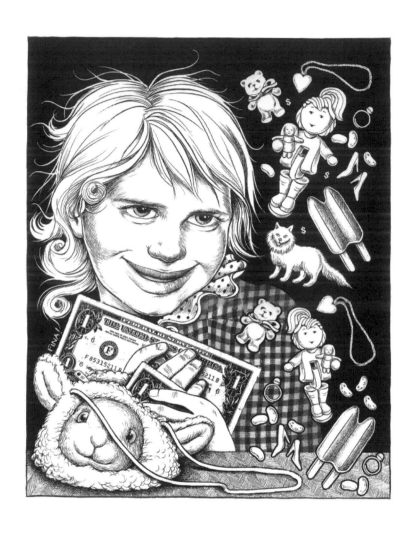

OTHER CHILDISH STORIES

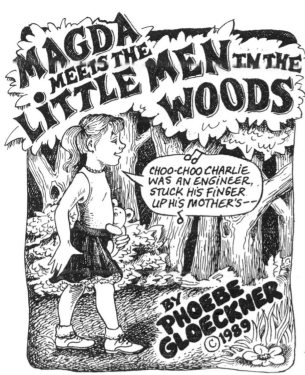

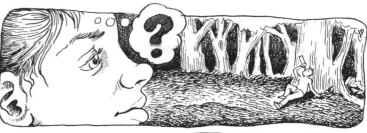

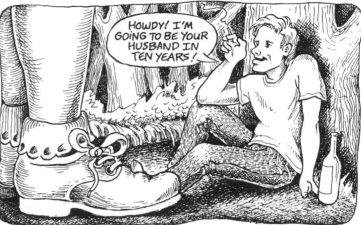

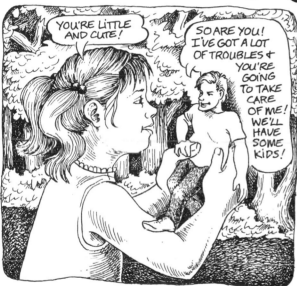

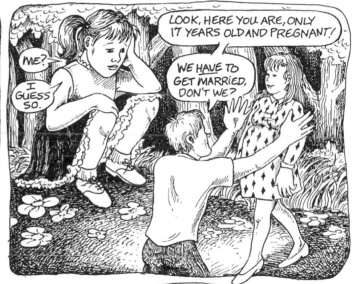

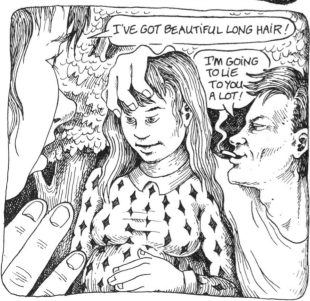

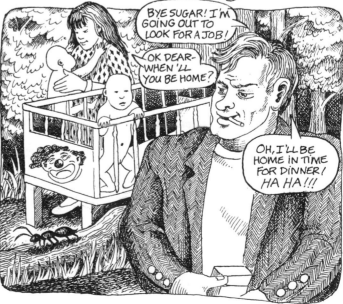

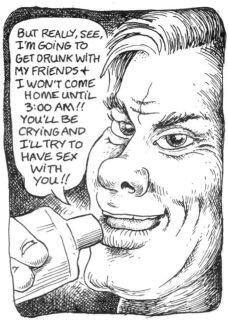

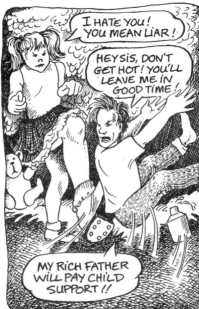

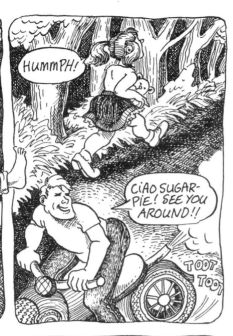

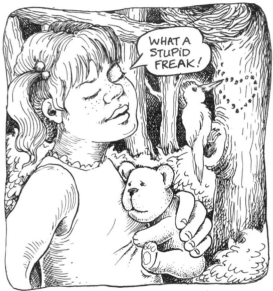

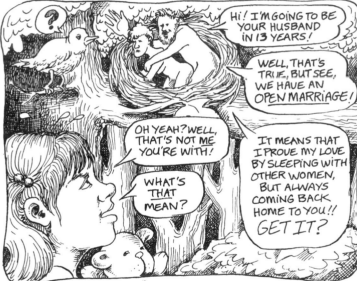

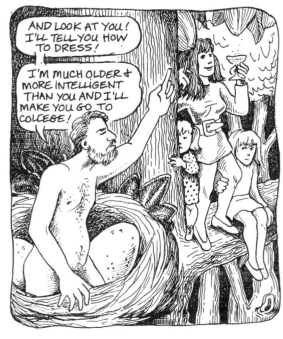

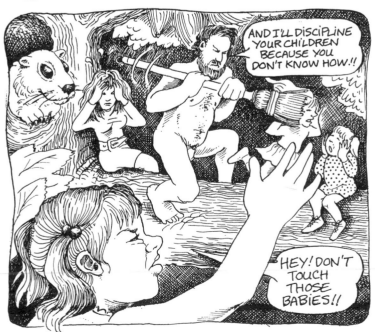

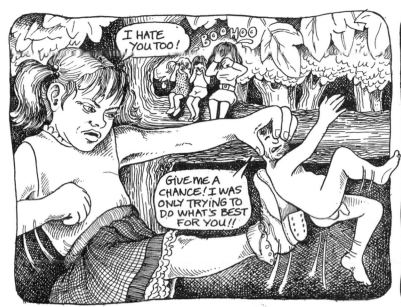

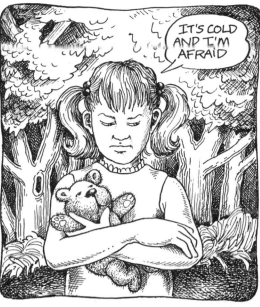

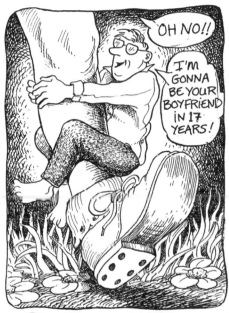

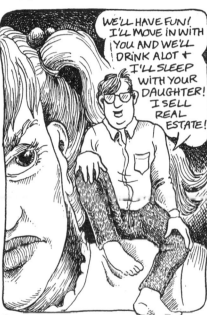

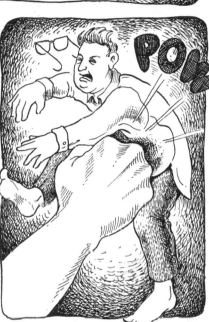

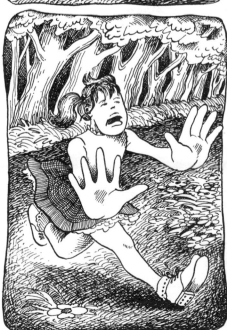

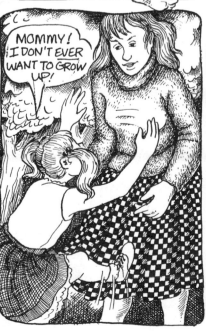

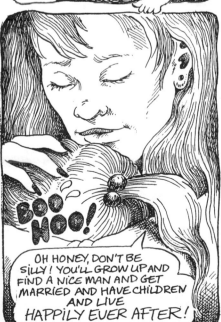

CAT LITTER CAPER

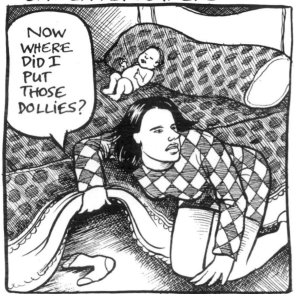

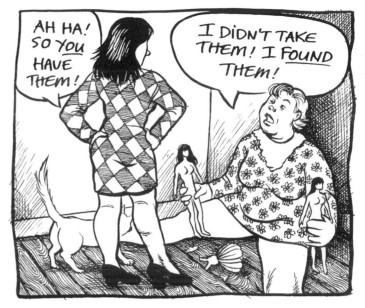

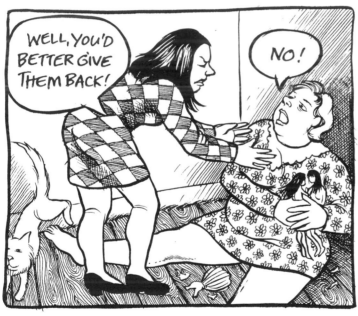

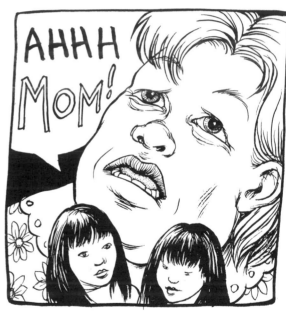

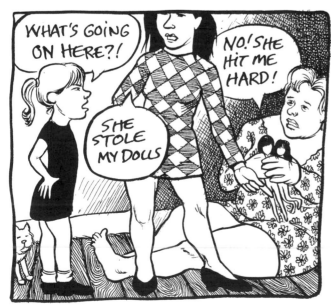

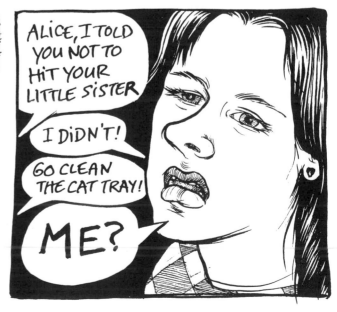

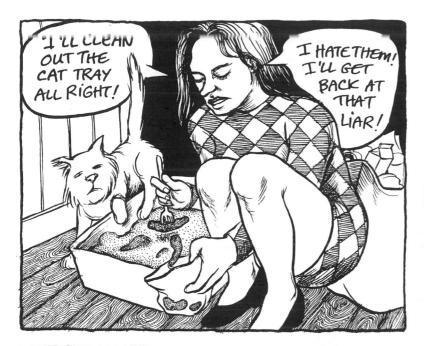

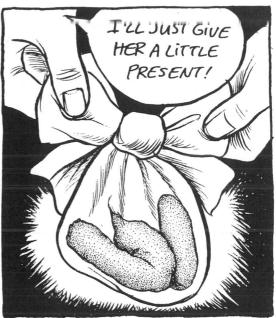

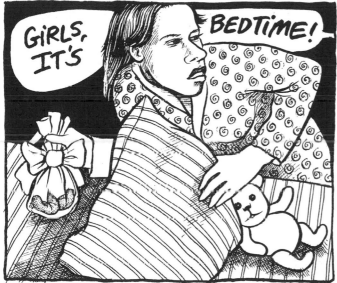

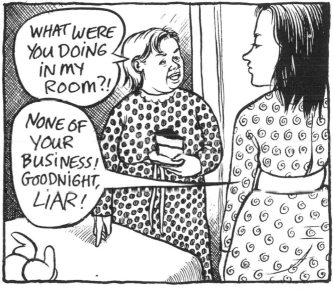

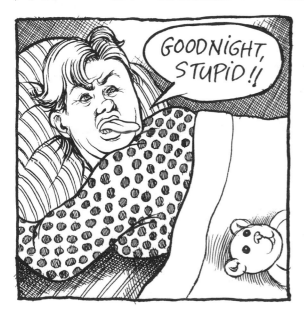

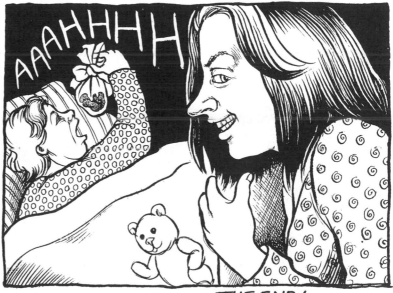

THE END!

FUN THINGS TO DO

SHADDUP.

THIS BONUS STORY concludes on p.3 frame 5 !!!!

MOMMA! KIN WE GIT DIS CEREAL?

SMEKKIES FREE MAZE!

WITH LITTLE GIRLS

by PHOEBE "Never gets over anything" GLOECKNER ©1993

MY STEPFATHER WAS BORN TO SCOTCH PEASANTRY BUT WHEN HE BECAME SUCESSFUL AND WEALTHY HE INSISTED THAT WE AFFECT THE BEHAVIOR OF LITTLE LADIES.

YOU GIRLS MUST SHARE A GLASS OF THIS MARVELOUS PINOT NOIR WITH ME. YOUR MOTHER WOULDN'T APPRECIATE ITS SUBTLETIES BUT YOU TWO ARE YOUNG AND CAN BE TRAINED

ANXIOUS TO PLEASE AND WANTING TO APPEAR TO BE SOPHISTICATED, I DRANK SOME WINE.

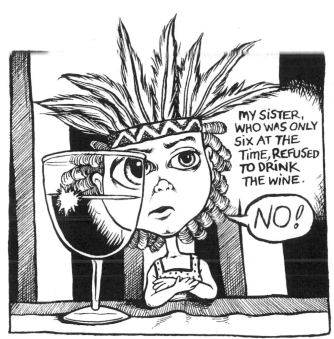

MY SISTER, WHO WAS ONLY SIX AT THE TIME, REFUSED TO DRINK THE WINE.

NO!

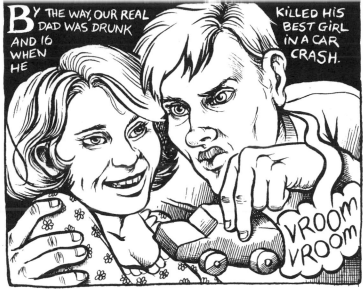

BY THE WAY, OUR REAL DAD WAS DRUNK AND 16 WHEN HE KILLED HIS BEST GIRL IN A CAR CRASH.

VROOM VROOM

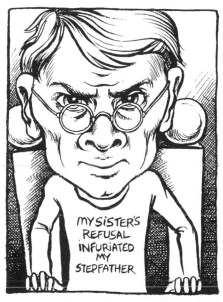

MY SISTER'S REFUSAL INFURIATED MY STEPFATHER

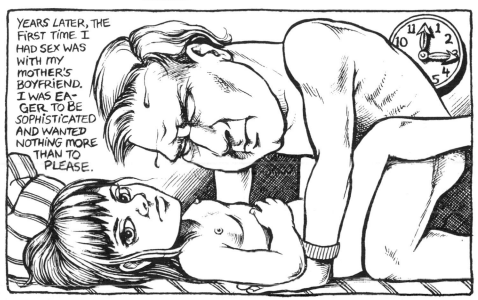

YEARS LATER, THE FIRST TIME I HAD SEX WAS WITH MY MOTHER'S BOYFRIEND. I WAS EAGER TO BE SOPHISTICATED AND WANTED NOTHING MORE THAN TO PLEASE.

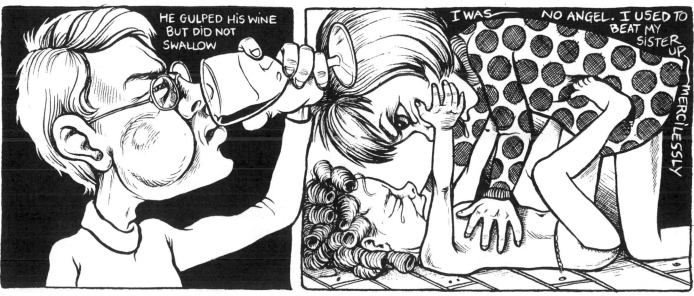

HE GULPED HIS WINE BUT DID NOT SWALLOW

I WAS NO ANGEL. I USED TO BEAT MY SISTER UP MERCILESSLY

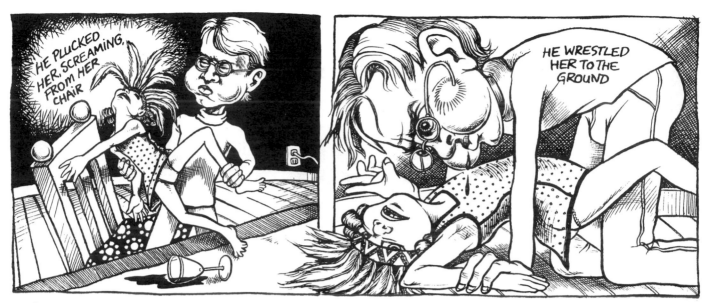

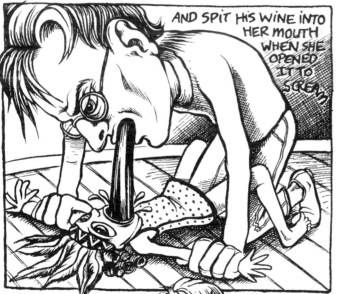

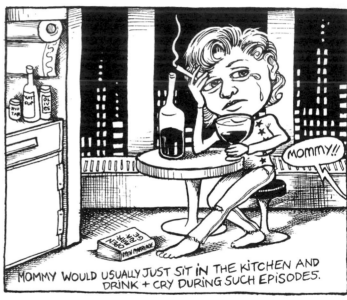

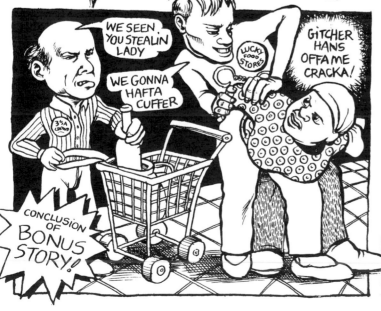

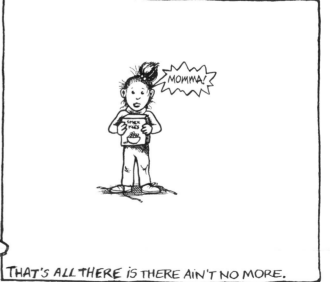

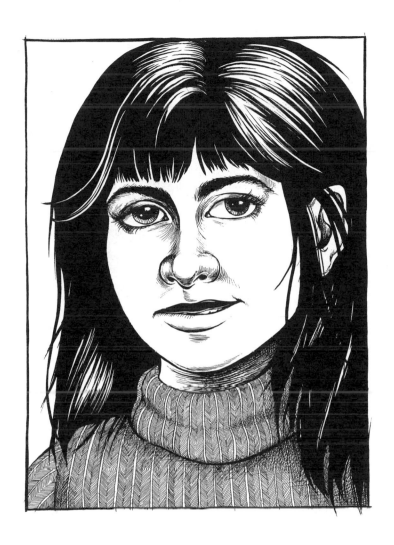

TEEN STORIES

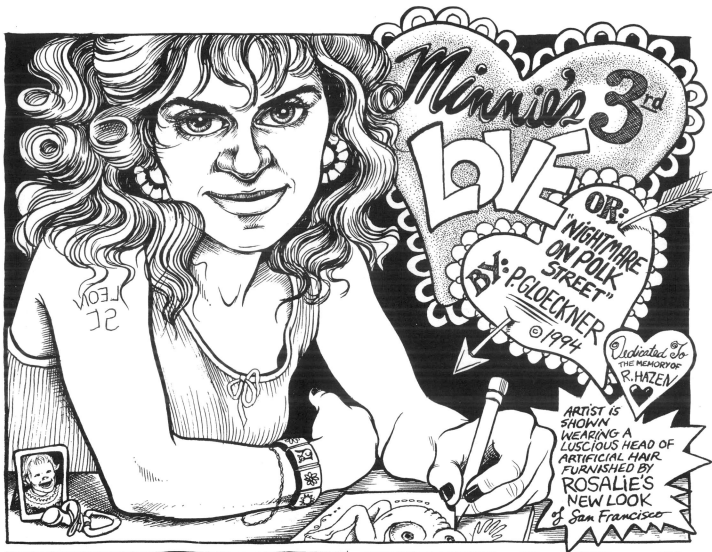

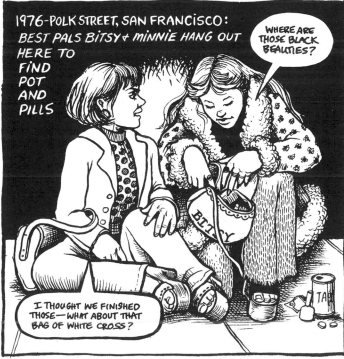

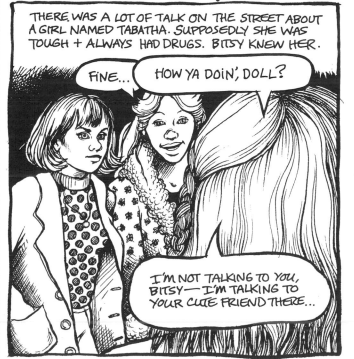

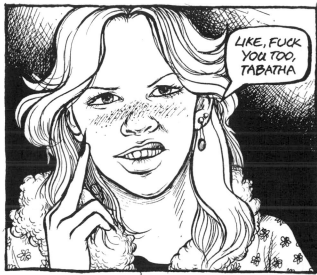

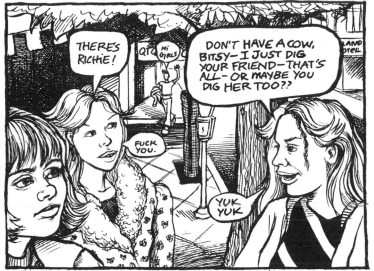

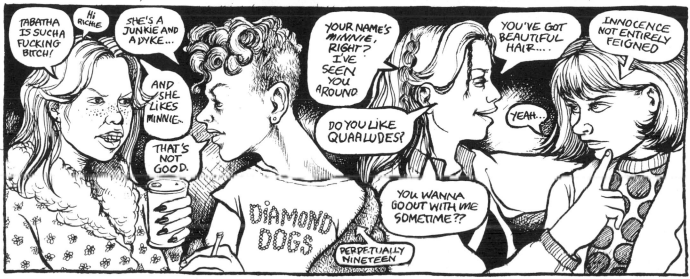

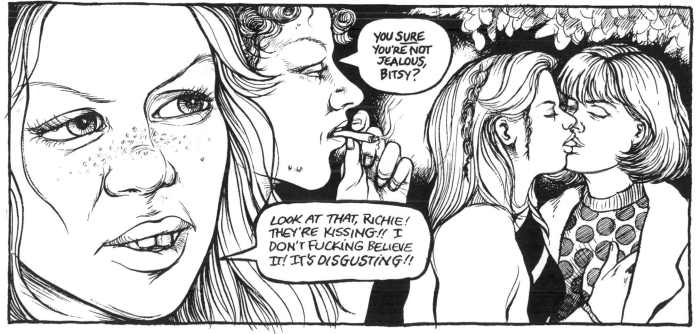

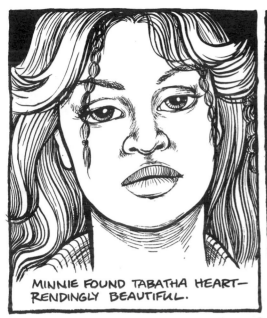

MINNIE FOUND TABATHA HEART-RENDINGLY BEAUTIFUL.

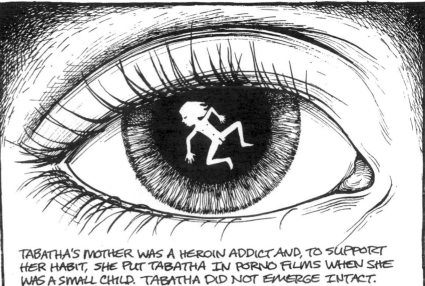

TABATHA'S MOTHER WAS A HEROIN ADDICT AND, TO SUPPORT HER HABIT, SHE PUT TABATHA IN PORNO FILMS WHEN SHE WAS A SMALL CHILD. TABATHA DID NOT EMERGE INTACT.

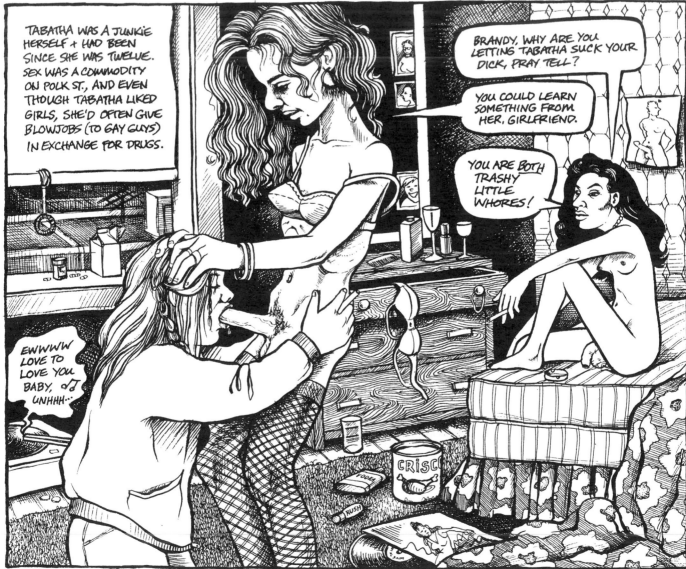

TABATHA WAS A JUNKIE HERSELF + HAD BEEN SINCE SHE WAS TWELVE. SEX WAS A COMMODITY ON POLK ST., AND EVEN THOUGH TABATHA LIKED GIRLS, SHE'D OFTEN GIVE BLOWJOBS (TO GAY GUYS) IN EXCHANGE FOR DRUGS.

EWWWW LOVE TO LOVE YOU BABY, ♪♩ UNHHH...

BRANDY, WHY ARE YOU LETTING TABATHA SUCK YOUR DICK, PRAY TELL?

YOU COULD LEARN SOMETHING FROM HER, GIRLFRIEND.

YOU ARE BOTH TRASHY LITTLE WHORES!

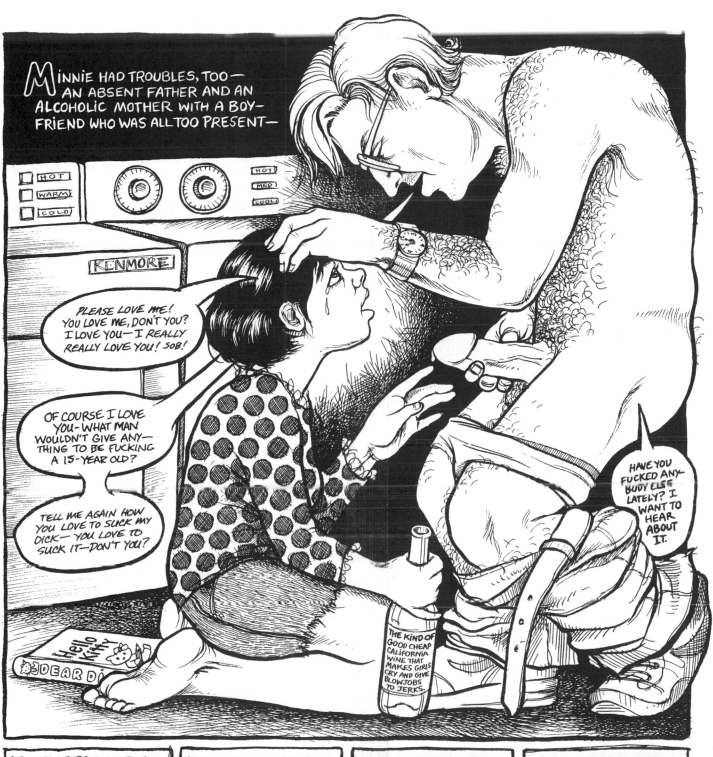

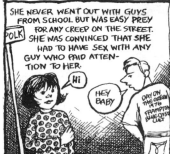

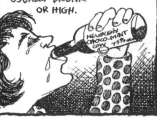

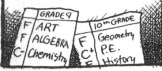

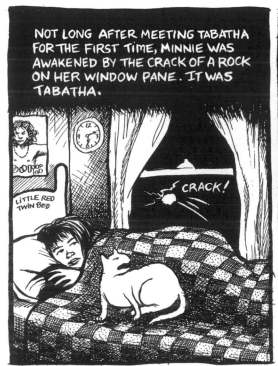

NOT LONG AFTER MEETING TABATHA FOR THE FIRST TIME, MINNIE WAS AWAKENED BY THE CRACK OF A ROCK ON HER WINDOW PANE. IT WAS TABATHA.

CRACK!

LITTLE RED TWIN BED

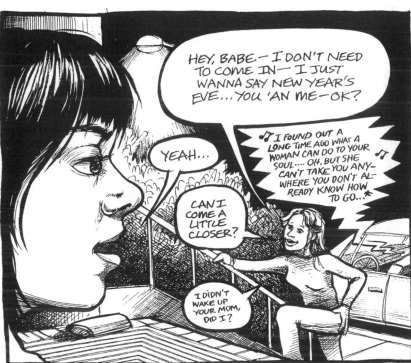

HEY, BABE — I DON'T NEED TO COME IN — I JUST WANNA SAY NEW YEAR'S EVE... YOU 'AN ME — OK?

YEAH...

CAN I COME A LITTLE CLOSER?

I DIDN'T WAKE UP YOUR MOM, DID I?

♪ I FOUND OUT A LONG TIME AGO WHAT A WOMAN CAN DO TO YOUR SOUL..... OH, BUT SHE CAN'T TAKE YOU ANY- WHERE YOU DON'T AL- READY KNOW HOW TO GO...* ♪

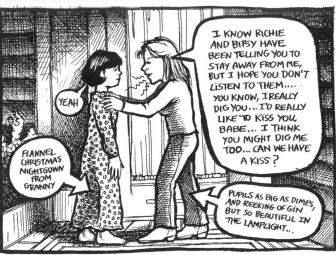

I KNOW RICHIE AND BITSY HAVE BEEN TELLING YOU TO STAY AWAY FROM ME, BUT I HOPE YOU DON'T LISTEN TO THEM..... YOU KNOW, I REALLY DIG YOU... I'D REALLY LIKE TO KISS YOU, BABE... I THINK YOU MIGHT DIG ME TOO... CAN WE HAVE A KISS?

YEAH

FLANNEL CHRISTMAS NIGHTGOWN FROM GRANNY

PUPILS AS BIG AS DIMES, AND REEKING OF GIN, BUT SO BEAUTIFUL IN THE LAMPLIGHT...

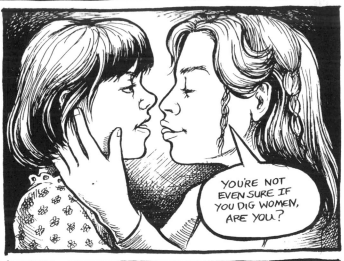

YOU'RE NOT EVEN SURE IF YOU DIG WOMEN, ARE YOU?

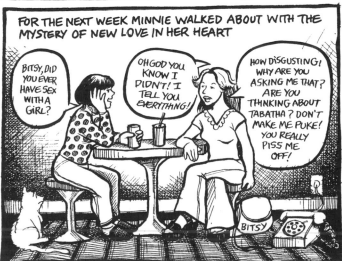

FOR THE NEXT WEEK MINNIE WALKED ABOUT WITH THE MYSTERY OF NEW LOVE IN HER HEART

BITSY, DID YOU EVER HAVE SEX WITH A GIRL?

OH GOD YOU KNOW I DIDN'T! I TELL YOU EVERYTHING!

HOW DISGUSTING! WHY ARE YOU ASKING ME THAT? ARE YOU THINKING ABOUT TABATHA? DON'T MAKE ME PUKE! YOU REALLY PISS ME OFF!

BITSY

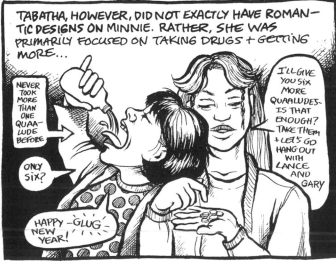

TABATHA, HOWEVER, DID NOT EXACTLY HAVE ROMAN- TIC DESIGNS ON MINNIE. RATHER, SHE WAS PRIMARILY FOCUSED ON TAKING DRUGS + GETTING MORE...

NEVER TOOK MORE THAN ONE QUAA- LUDE BEFORE

ONLY SIX?

HAPPY —GLUG— NEW YEAR!

I'LL GIVE YOU SIX MORE QUAALUDES— IS THAT ENOUGH? TAKE THEM + LET'S GO HANG OUT WITH LANCE AND GARY

* "PEACEFUL FEELING," by the EAGLES.

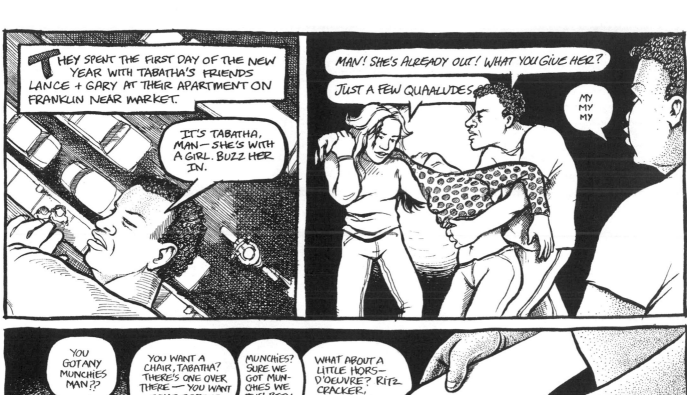

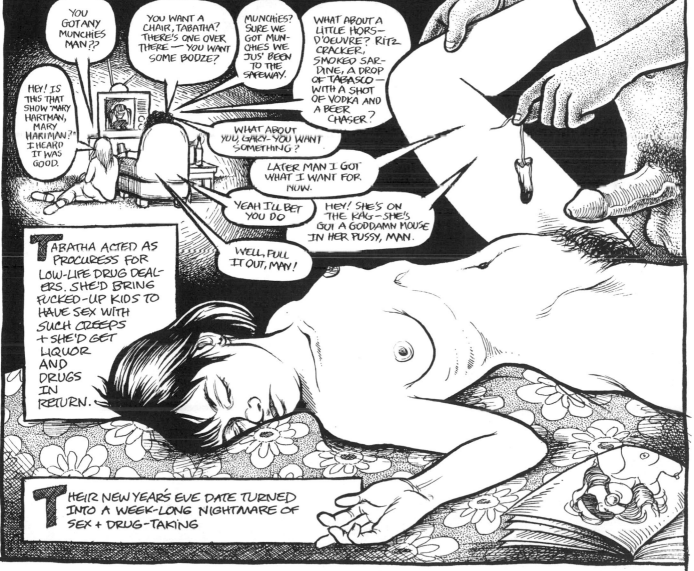

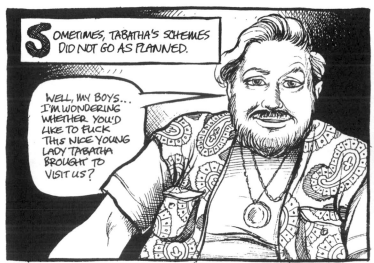

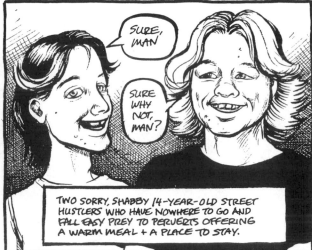

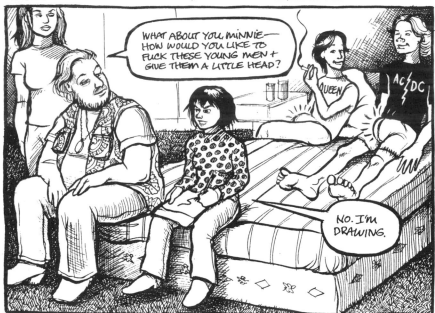

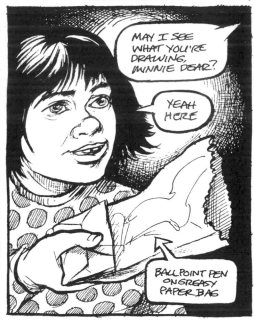

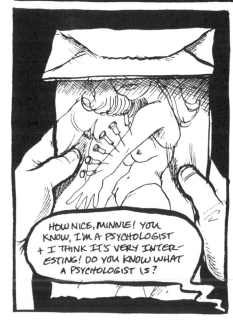

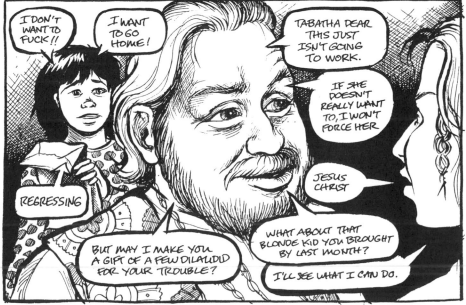

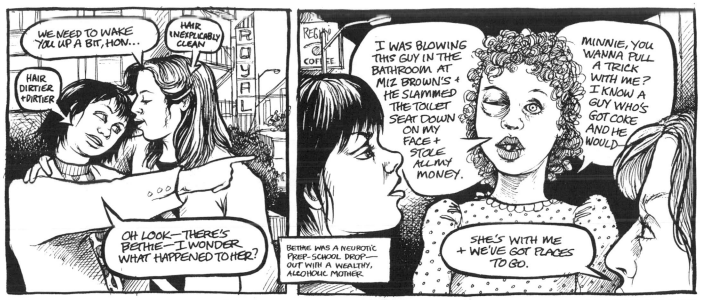

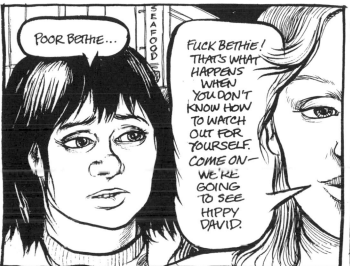

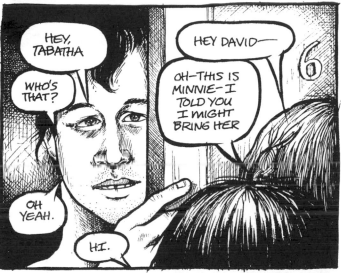

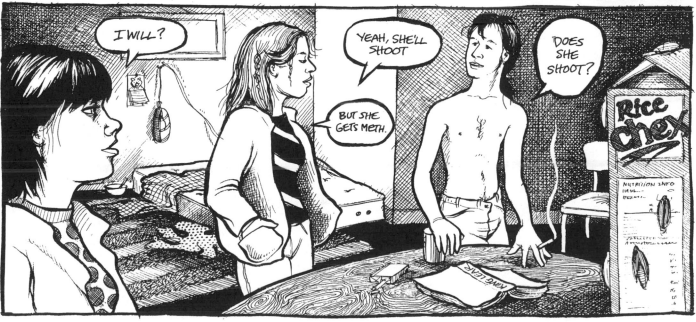

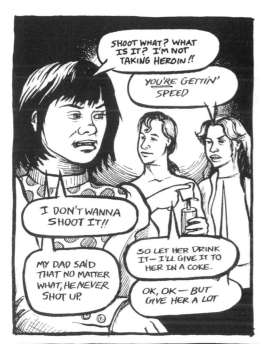

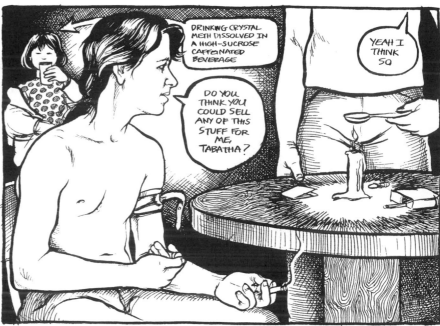

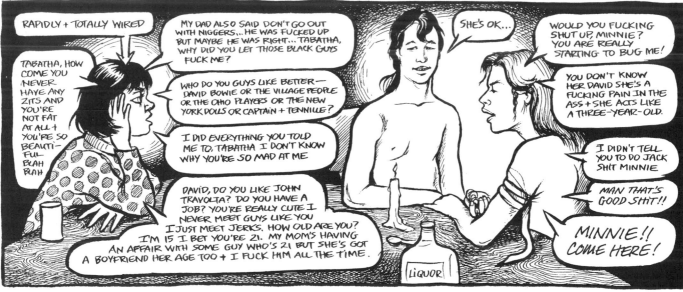

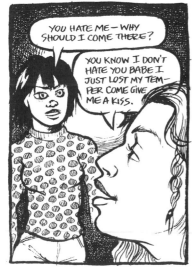

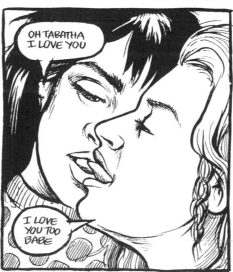

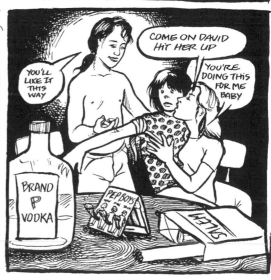

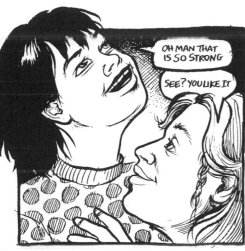

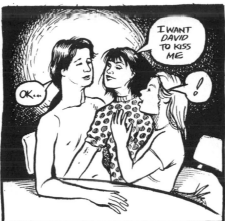

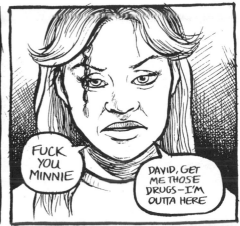

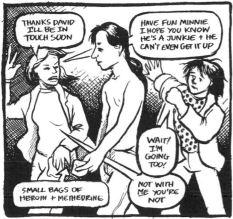

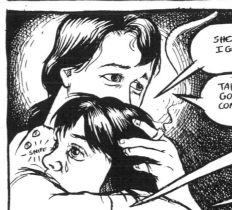

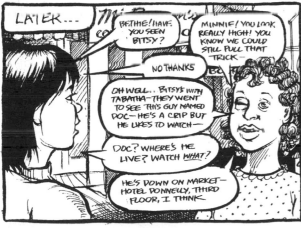

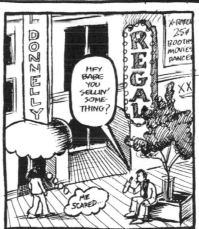

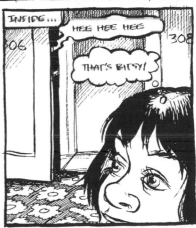

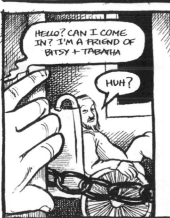

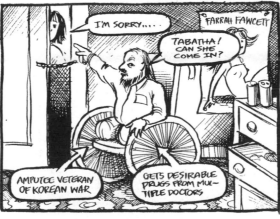

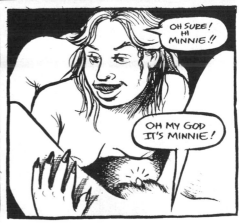

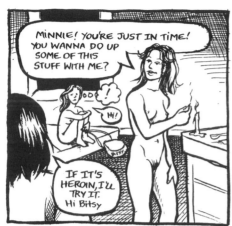

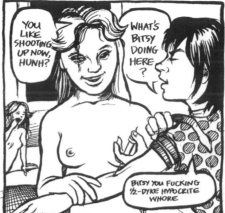

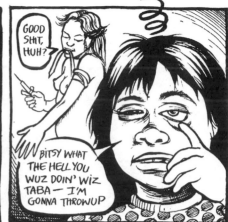

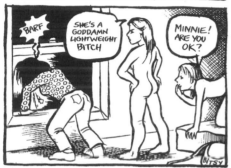

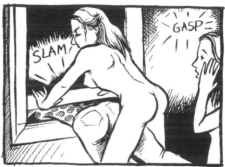

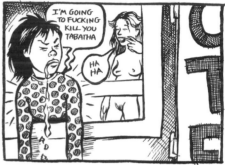

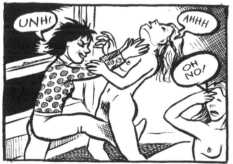

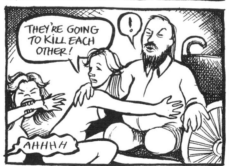

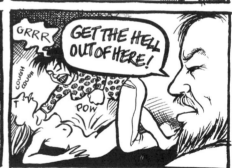

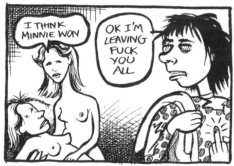

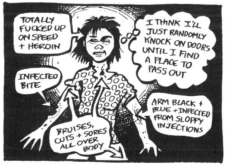

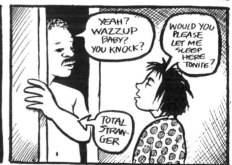

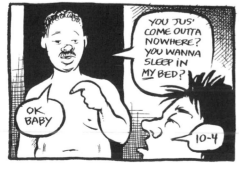

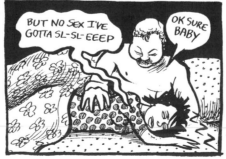

AND SO ON....

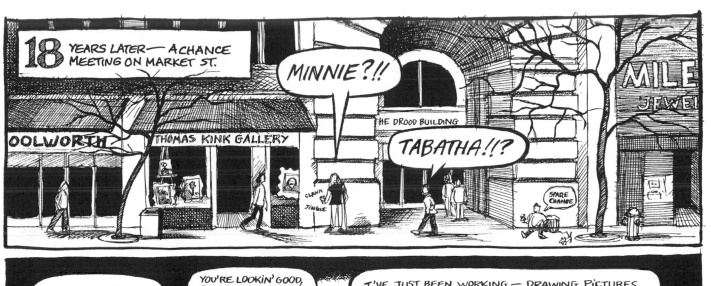

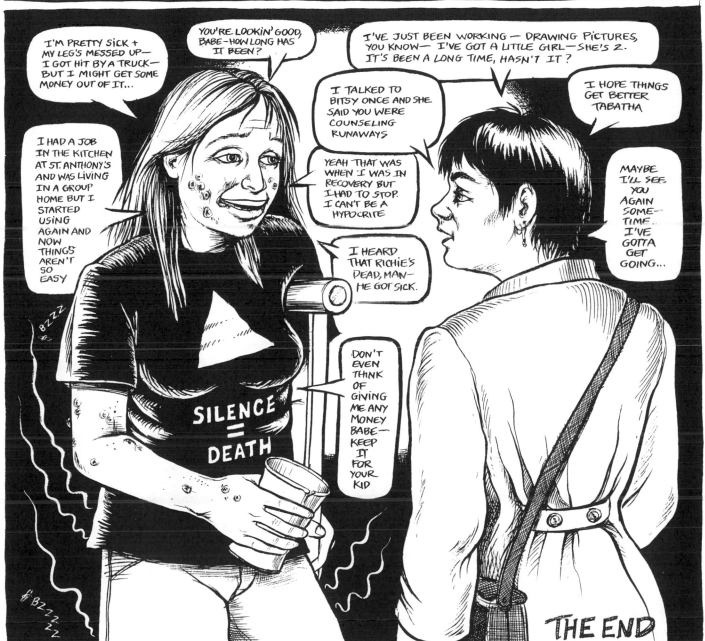

* drawn at age sixteen

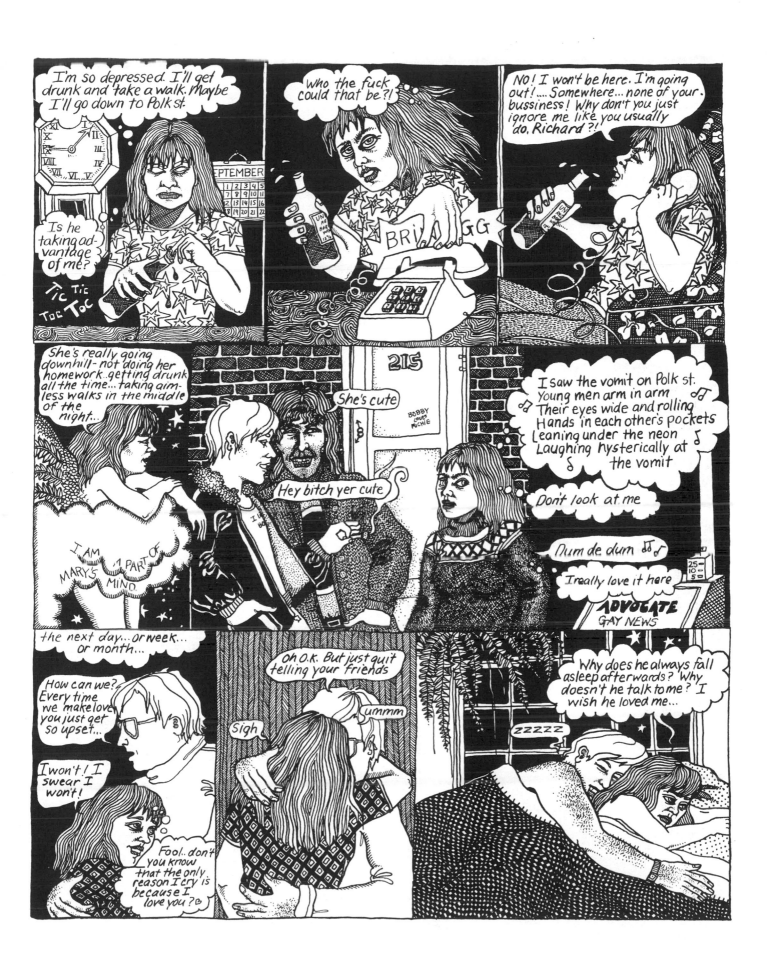

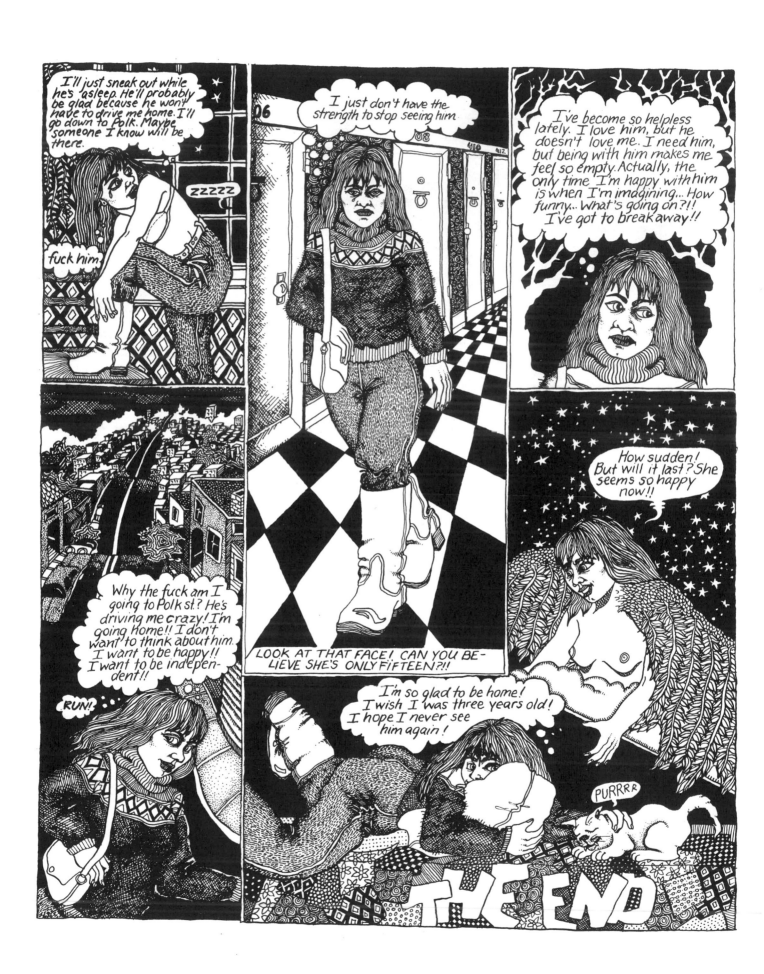

Vocational Training

P. Gloeckner

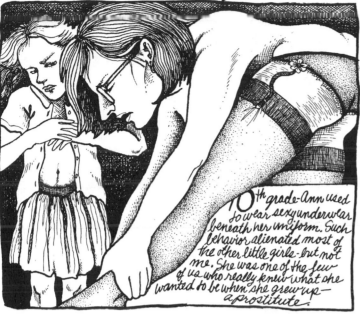

10th grade-Ann used to wear sexy underwear beneath her uniform. Such behavior alienated most of the other little girls-but not me. She was one of the few of us who really knew what she wanted to be when she grew up—a prostitute.

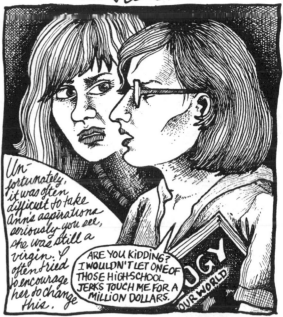

Unfortunately, it was often difficult to take Ann's aspirations seriously-you see, she was still a virgin. I often tried to encourage her to change this.

ARE YOU KIDDING? I WOULDN'T LET ONE OF THOSE HIGH SCHOOL JERKS TOUCH ME FOR A MILLION DOLLARS.

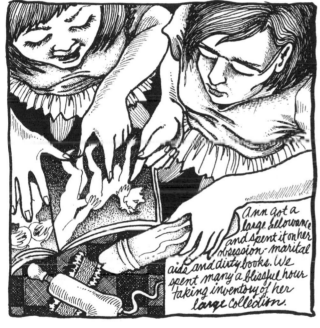

Ann got a large allowance and spent it on her obsession-marital aids and dirty books. We spent many a blissful hour taking inventory of her large collection.

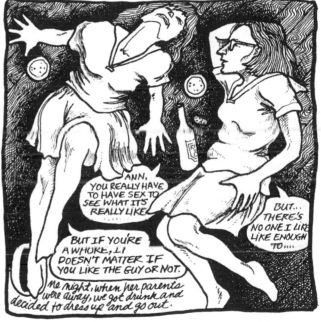

ANN, YOU REALLY HAVE TO HAVE SEX TO SEE WHAT IT'S REALLY LIKE!

BUT... THERE'S NO ONE I LIKE LIKE ENOUGH TO....

BUT IF YOU'RE A WHORE, IT DOESN'T MATTER IF YOU LIKE THE GUY OR NOT.

One night, when her parents were away, we got drunk and decided to dress up and go out.

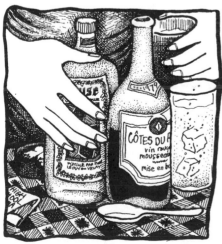

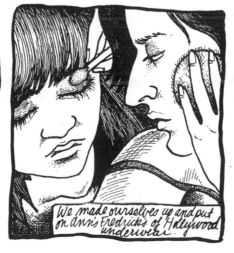

We made ourselves up and put on Ann's Fredrick's of Hollywood underwear.

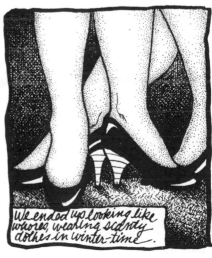

We ended up looking like whores, wearing scanty clothes in winter-time.

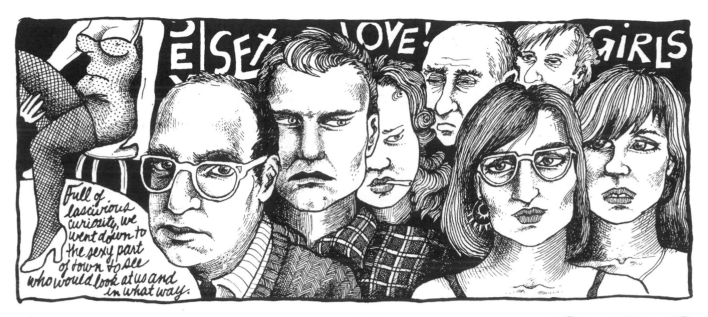

Full of lascivious curiosity, we went down to the sexy part of town to see who would look at us and in what way.

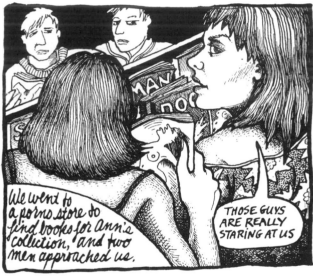

We went to a porno store to find books for Anne's collection, and two men approached us.

THOSE GUYS ARE REALLY STARING AT US

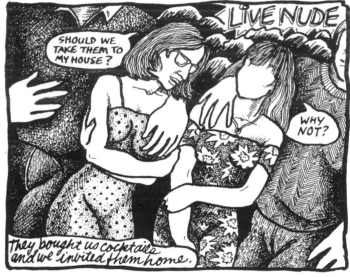

SHOULD WE TAKE THEM TO MY HOUSE?

WHY NOT?

They bought us cocktails and we invited them home.

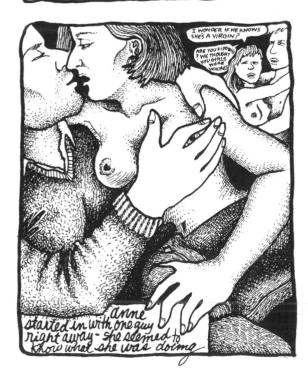

I WONDER IF HE KNOWS SHE'S A VIRGIN?

ARE YOU KIDDING? WE THOUGHT YOU GIRLS WERE WHORES

Anne started in with one guy right away - she seemed to know what she was doing

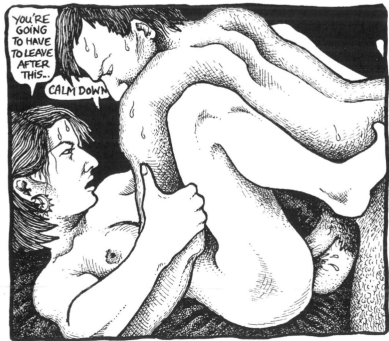

YOU'RE GOING TO HAVE TO LEAVE AFTER THIS..

CALM DOWN

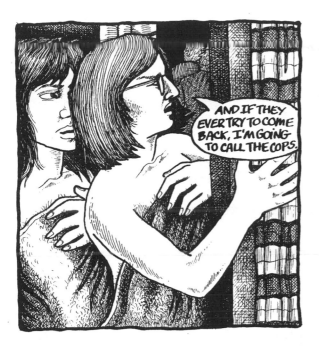

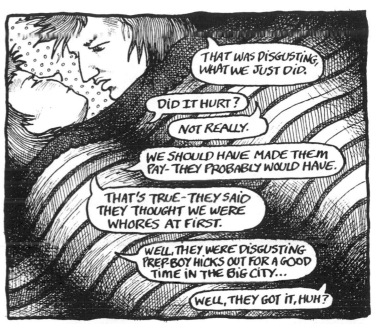

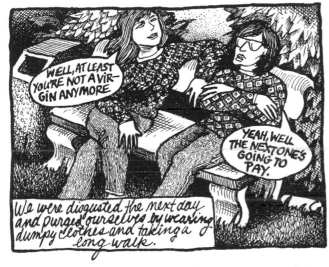

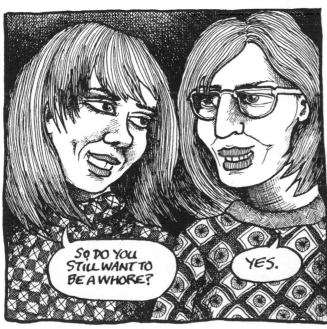

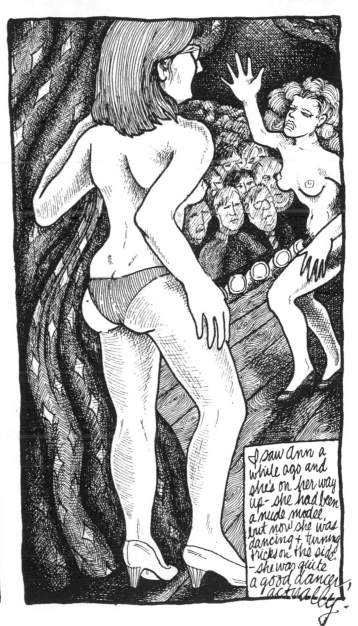

The girl from A DIFFERENT WORLD

by PHOEBE GLOECKNER ©1996

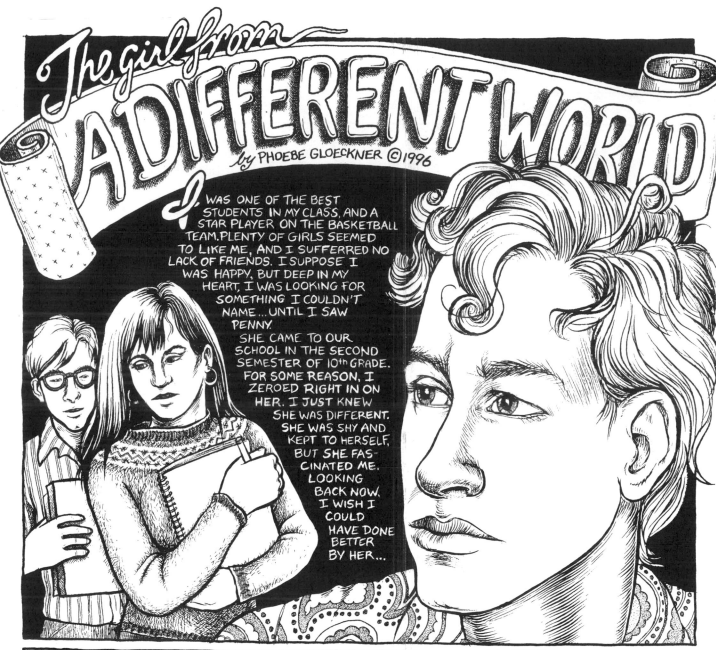

I WAS ONE OF THE BEST STUDENTS IN MY CLASS, AND A STAR PLAYER ON THE BASKETBALL TEAM. PLENTY OF GIRLS SEEMED TO LIKE ME, AND I SUFFERRED NO LACK OF FRIENDS. I SUPPOSE I WAS HAPPY, BUT DEEP IN MY HEART, I WAS LOOKING FOR SOMETHING I COULDN'T NAME... UNTIL I SAW PENNY.

SHE CAME TO OUR SCHOOL IN THE SECOND SEMESTER OF 10th GRADE. FOR SOME REASON, I ZEROED RIGHT IN ON HER. I JUST KNEW SHE WAS DIFFERENT. SHE WAS SHY AND KEPT TO HERSELF, BUT SHE FAS-CINATED ME. LOOKING BACK NOW, I WISH I COULD HAVE DONE BETTER BY HER...

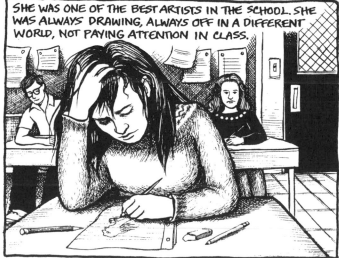

SHE WAS ONE OF THE BEST ARTISTS IN THE SCHOOL. SHE WAS ALWAYS DRAWING, ALWAYS OFF IN A DIFFERENT WORLD, NOT PAYING ATTENTION IN CLASS.

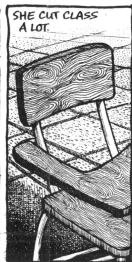

SHE CUT CLASS A LOT.

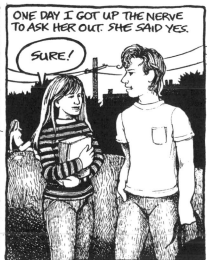

ONE DAY I GOT UP THE NERVE TO ASK HER OUT. SHE SAID YES.

SURE!

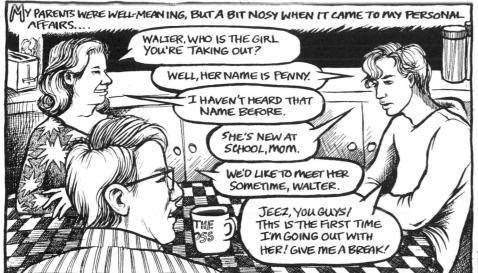

MY PARENTS WERE WELL-MEANING, BUT A BIT NOSY WHEN IT CAME TO MY PERSONAL AFFAIRS....

WALTER, WHO IS THE GIRL YOU'RE TAKING OUT?

WELL, HER NAME IS PENNY.

I HAVEN'T HEARD THAT NAME BEFORE.

SHE'S NEW AT SCHOOL, MOM.

WE'D LIKE TO MEET HER SOMETIME, WALTER.

JEEZ, YOU GUYS! THIS IS THE FIRST TIME I'M GOING OUT WITH HER! GIVE ME A BREAK!

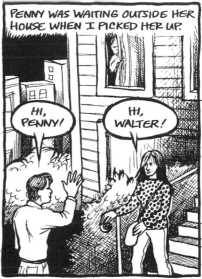

PENNY WAS WAITING OUTSIDE HER HOUSE WHEN I PICKED HER UP.

HI, PENNY!

HI, WALTER!

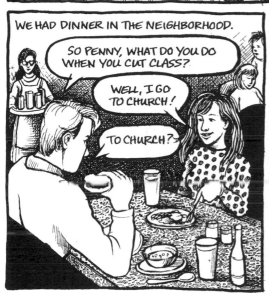

WE HAD DINNER IN THE NEIGHBORHOOD.

SO PENNY, WHAT DO YOU DO WHEN YOU CUT CLASS?

WELL, I GO TO CHURCH!

TO CHURCH?

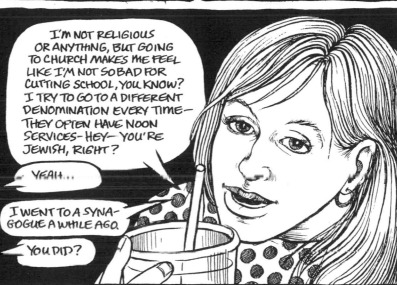

I'M NOT RELIGIOUS OR ANYTHING, BUT GOING TO CHURCH MAKES ME FEEL LIKE I'M NOT SO BAD FOR CUTTING SCHOOL, YOU KNOW? I TRY TO GO TO A DIFFERENT DENOMINATION EVERY TIME— THEY OFTEN HAVE NOON SERVICES- HEY— YOU'RE JEWISH, RIGHT?

YEAH...

I WENT TO A SYNA- GOGUE A WHILE AGO.

YOU DID?

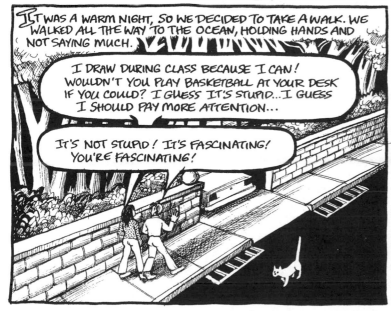

IT WAS A WARM NIGHT, SO WE DECIDED TO TAKE A WALK. WE WALKED ALL THE WAY TO THE OCEAN, HOLDING HANDS AND NOT SAYING MUCH.

I DRAW DURING CLASS BECAUSE I CAN! WOULDN'T YOU PLAY BASKETBALL AT YOUR DESK IF YOU COULD? I GUESS IT'S STUPID...I GUESS I SHOULD PAY MORE ATTENTION...

IT'S NOT STUPID! IT'S FASCINATING! YOU'RE FASCINATING!

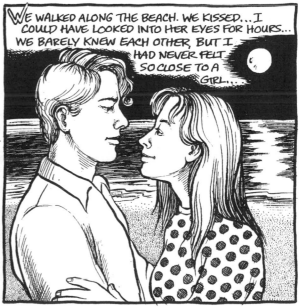

WE WALKED ALONG THE BEACH. WE KISSED...I COULD HAVE LOOKED INTO HER EYES FOR HOURS... WE BARELY KNEW EACH OTHER, BUT I HAD NEVER FELT SO CLOSE TO A GIRL...

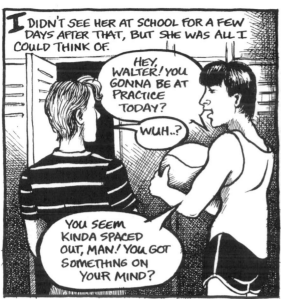

I DIDN'T SEE HER AT SCHOOL FOR A FEW DAYS AFTER THAT, BUT SHE WAS ALL I COULD THINK OF.

HEY, WALTER! YOU GONNA BE AT PRACTICE TODAY?

WUH..?

YOU SEEM KINDA SPACED OUT, MAN! YOU GOT SOMETHING ON YOUR MIND?

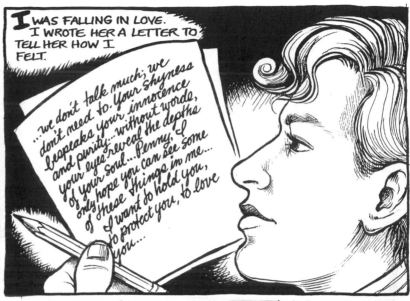

I WAS FALLING IN LOVE. I WROTE HER A LETTER TO TELL HER HOW I FELT.

...we don't talk much; we don't need to. Your shyness bespeaks your innocence and purity... without words, your eyes reveal the depths of your soul... Penny, I only hope you can see some of these things in me... I want to hold you, to protect you, to love you...

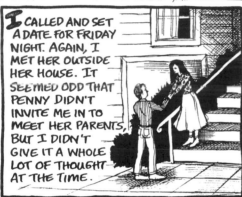

I CALLED AND SET A DATE FOR FRIDAY NIGHT. AGAIN, I MET HER OUTSIDE HER HOUSE. IT SEEMED ODD THAT PENNY DIDN'T INVITE ME IN TO MEET HER PARENTS, BUT I DIDN'T GIVE IT A WHOLE LOT OF THOUGHT AT THE TIME.

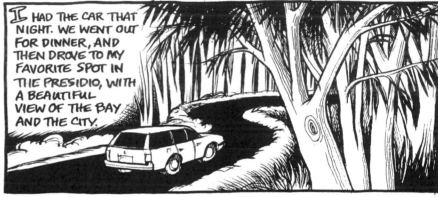

I HAD THE CAR THAT NIGHT. WE WENT OUT FOR DINNER, AND THEN DROVE TO MY FAVORITE SPOT IN THE PRESIDIO, WITH A BEAUTIFUL VIEW OF THE BAY AND THE CITY.

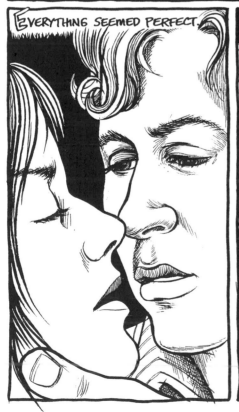

EVERYTHING SEEMED PERFECT.

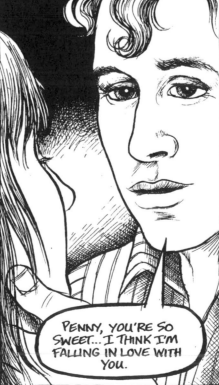

PENNY, YOU'RE SO SWEET... I THINK I'M FALLING IN LOVE WITH YOU.

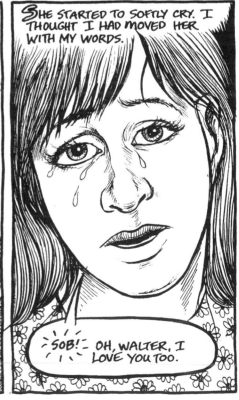

SHE STARTED TO SOFTLY CRY. I THOUGHT I HAD MOVED HER WITH MY WORDS.

SOB! OH, WALTER, I LOVE YOU TOO.

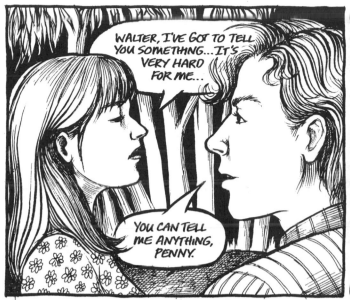

WALTER, I'VE GOT TO TELL YOU SOMETHING...IT'S VERY HARD FOR ME...

YOU CAN TELL ME ANYTHING, PENNY.

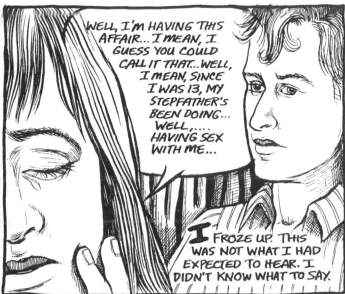

WELL, I'M HAVING THIS AFFAIR...I MEAN, I GUESS YOU COULD CALL IT THAT...WELL, I MEAN, SINCE I WAS 13, MY STEPFATHER'S BEEN DOING... WELL,...... HAVING SEX WITH ME...

I FROZE UP. THIS WAS NOT WHAT I HAD EXPECTED TO HEAR. I DIDN'T KNOW WHAT TO SAY.

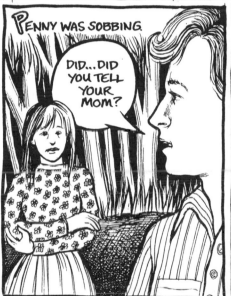

PENNY WAS SOBBING.

DID...DID YOU TELL YOUR MOM?

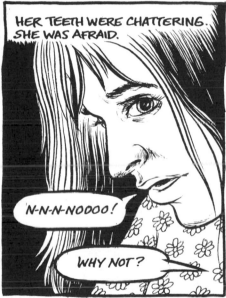

HER TEETH WERE CHATTERING. SHE WAS AFRAID.

N-N-N-NOOOO!

WHY NOT?

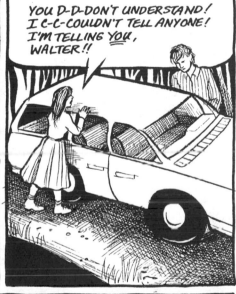

YOU D-D-DON'T UNDERSTAND! I C-C-COULDN'T TELL ANYONE! I'M TELLING YOU, WALTER!!

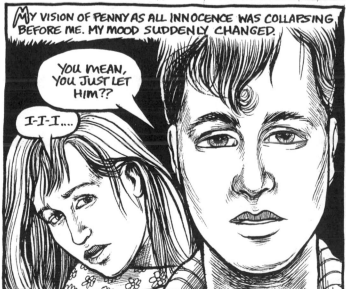

MY VISION OF PENNY AS ALL INNOCENCE WAS COLLAPSING BEFORE ME. MY MOOD SUDDENLY CHANGED.

YOU MEAN, YOU JUST LET HIM??

I-I-I....

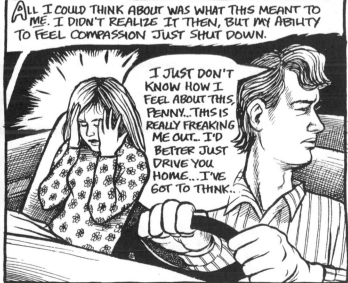

ALL I COULD THINK ABOUT WAS WHAT THIS MEANT TO ME. I DIDN'T REALIZE IT THEN, BUT MY ABILITY TO FEEL COMPASSION JUST SHUT DOWN.

I JUST DON'T KNOW HOW I FEEL ABOUT THIS, PENNY...THIS IS REALLY FREAKING ME OUT...I'D BETTER JUST DRIVE YOU HOME...I'VE GOT TO THINK..

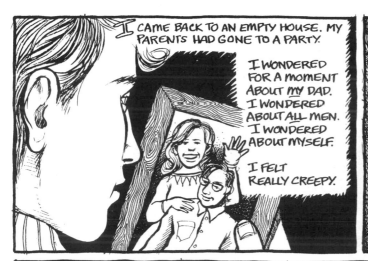

I CAME BACK TO AN EMPTY HOUSE. MY PARENTS HAD GONE TO A PARTY.

I WONDERED FOR A MOMENT ABOUT *MY* DAD. I WONDERED ABOUT ALL MEN. I WONDERED ABOUT MYSELF.

I FELT REALLY CREEPY.

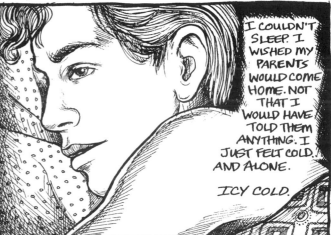

I COULDN'T SLEEP. I WISHED MY PARENTS WOULD COME HOME. NOT THAT I WOULD HAVE TOLD THEM ANYTHING. I JUST FELT COLD, AND ALONE.

ICY COLD.

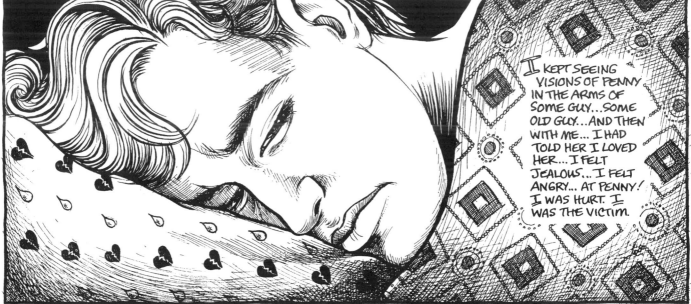

I KEPT SEEING VISIONS OF PENNY IN THE ARMS OF SOME GUY...SOME OLD GUY...AND THEN WITH ME... I HAD TOLD HER I LOVED HER.... I FELT JEALOUS... I FELT ANGRY... AT PENNY! I WAS HURT. I WAS THE VICTIM.

I'D SEE HER VULNERABLE CRYING FORM...

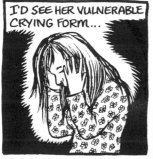

BUT IT WOULD BE RE-PLACED WITH SOME HOR-RIFYING IMAGE OF HER SUBMITTING TO THAT MAN

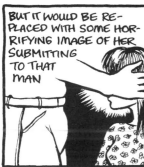

AND I'D SEE HER AS WEAK, NOT DE-SERVING MY LOVE.

PASS THE POTATOES, PENNY DEAR.

YES, DAD

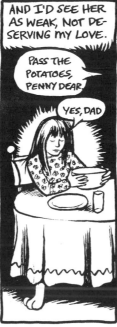

I'D SEE HER IN MY ARMS AGAIN, I COULD ALMOST FEEL HER....

I LOVE YOU, TOO, WALTER

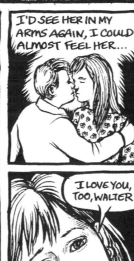

WHO WAS THAT MAN?

A SLEEZE...

A STUD...

A NORMAL-LOOKING PATERNAL TYPE?

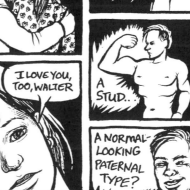

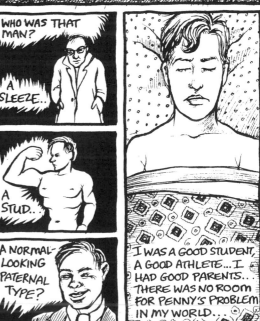

I WAS A GOOD STUDENT, A GOOD ATHLETE... I HAD GOOD PARENTS... THERE WAS NO ROOM FOR PENNY'S PROBLEM IN MY WORLD....

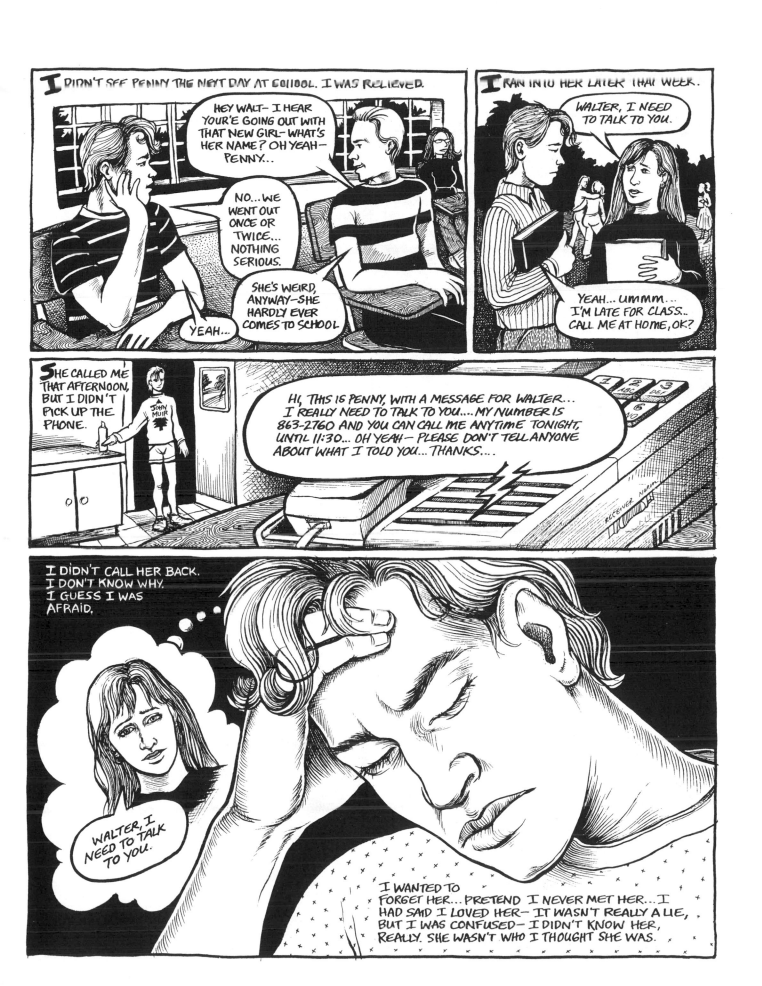

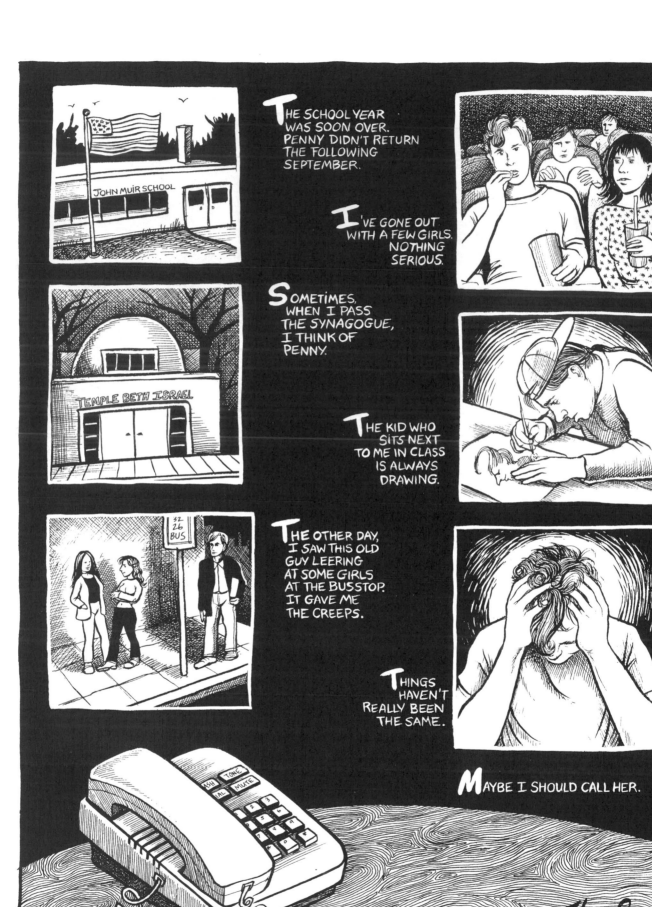

THE SCHOOL YEAR WAS SOON OVER. PENNY DIDN'T RETURN THE FOLLOWING SEPTEMBER.

I'VE GONE OUT WITH A FEW GIRLS. NOTHING SERIOUS.

SOMETIMES, WHEN I PASS THE SYNAGOGUE, I THINK OF PENNY.

THE KID WHO SITS NEXT TO ME IN CLASS IS ALWAYS DRAWING.

THE OTHER DAY, I SAW THIS OLD GUY LEERING AT SOME GIRLS AT THE BUSSTOP. IT GAVE ME THE CREEPS.

THINGS HAVEN'T REALLY BEEN THE SAME.

MAYBE I SHOULD CALL HER.

The End

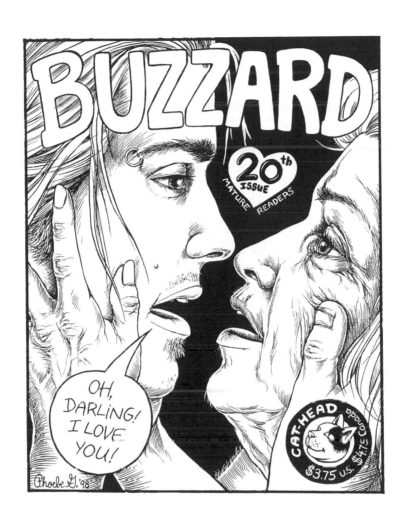

GROWN-UP STORIES

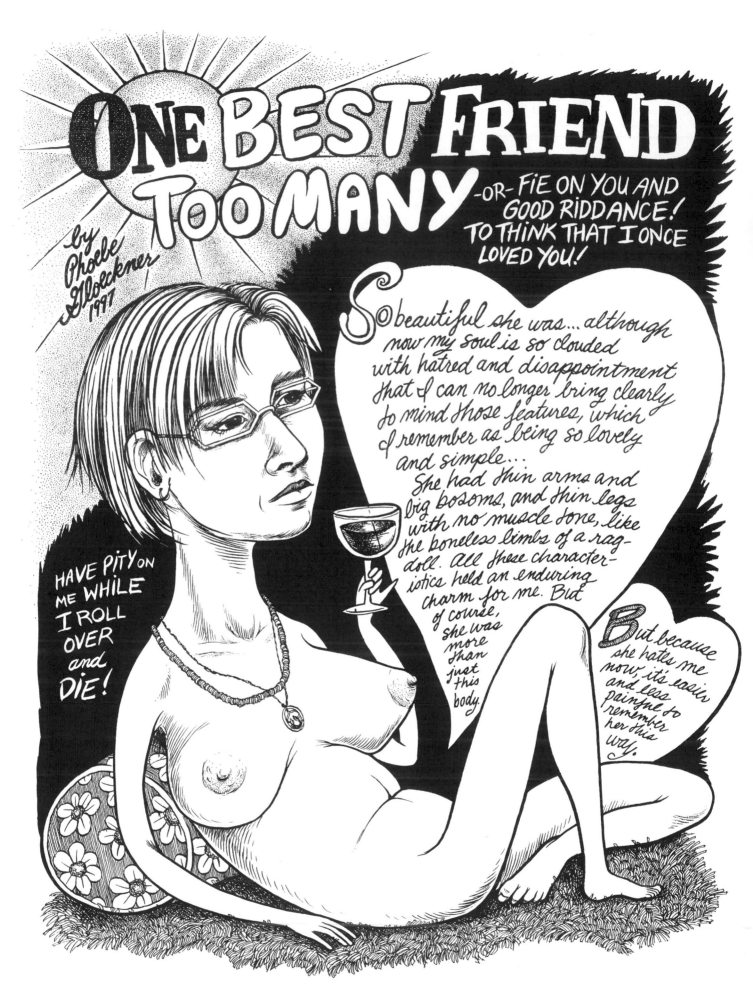

ONE BEST FRIEND TOO MANY

-OR- FIE ON YOU AND GOOD RIDDANCE! TO THINK THAT I ONCE LOVED YOU!

by Phoebe Gloeckner 1997

HAVE PITY ON ME WHILE I ROLL OVER and DIE!

So beautiful she was.... although now my soul is so clouded with hatred and disappointment that I can no longer bring clearly to mind those features, which I remember as being so lovely and simple...

She had thin arms and big bosoms, and thin legs with no muscle tone, like the boneless limbs of a ragdoll. All these characteristics held an enduring charm for me. But of course, she was more than just this body.

But because she hates me now, it's easier and less painful to remember her this way.

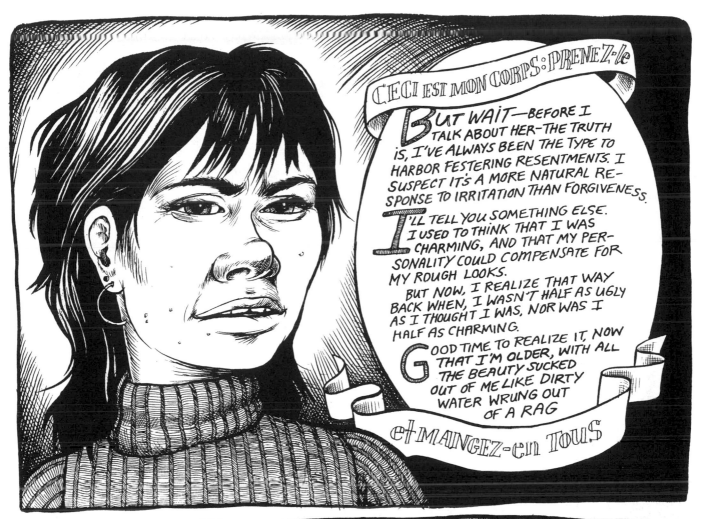

CECI EST MON CORPS : PRENEZ-le

BUT WAIT—BEFORE I TALK ABOUT HER—THE TRUTH IS, I'VE ALWAYS BEEN THE TYPE TO HARBOR FESTERING RESENTMENTS. I SUSPECT IT'S A MORE NATURAL RESPONSE TO IRRITATION THAN FORGIVENESS.

I'LL TELL YOU SOMETHING ELSE. I USED TO THINK THAT I WAS CHARMING, AND THAT MY PERSONALITY COULD COMPENSATE FOR MY ROUGH LOOKS.

BUT NOW, I REALIZE THAT WAY BACK WHEN, I WASN'T HALF AS UGLY AS I THOUGHT I WAS, NOR WAS I HALF AS CHARMING.

GOOD TIME TO REALIZE IT, NOW THAT I'M OLDER, WITH ALL THE BEAUTY SUCKED OUT OF ME LIKE DIRTY WATER WRUNG OUT OF A RAG

et MANGEZ-en TOUS

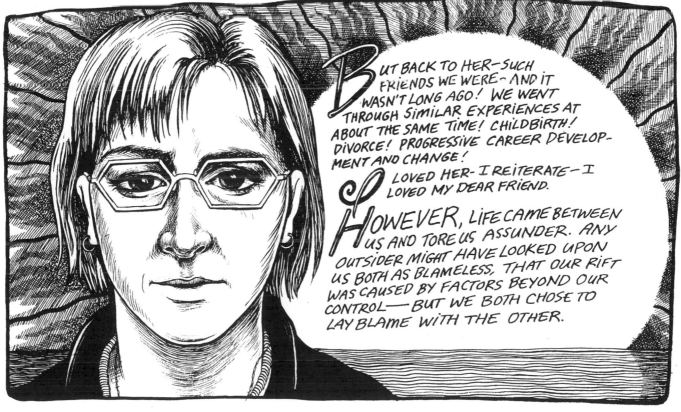

BUT BACK TO HER—SUCH FRIENDS WE WERE—AND IT WASN'T LONG AGO! WE WENT THROUGH SIMILAR EXPERIENCES AT ABOUT THE SAME TIME! CHILDBIRTH! DIVORCE! PROGRESSIVE CAREER DEVELOPMENT AND CHANGE!

I LOVED HER—I REITERATE—I LOVED MY DEAR FRIEND.

HOWEVER, LIFE CAME BETWEEN US AND TORE US ASSUNDER. ANY OUTSIDER MIGHT HAVE LOOKED UPON US BOTH AS BLAMELESS, THAT OUR RIFT WAS CAUSED BY FACTORS BEYOND OUR CONTROL—BUT WE BOTH CHOSE TO LAY BLAME WITH THE OTHER.

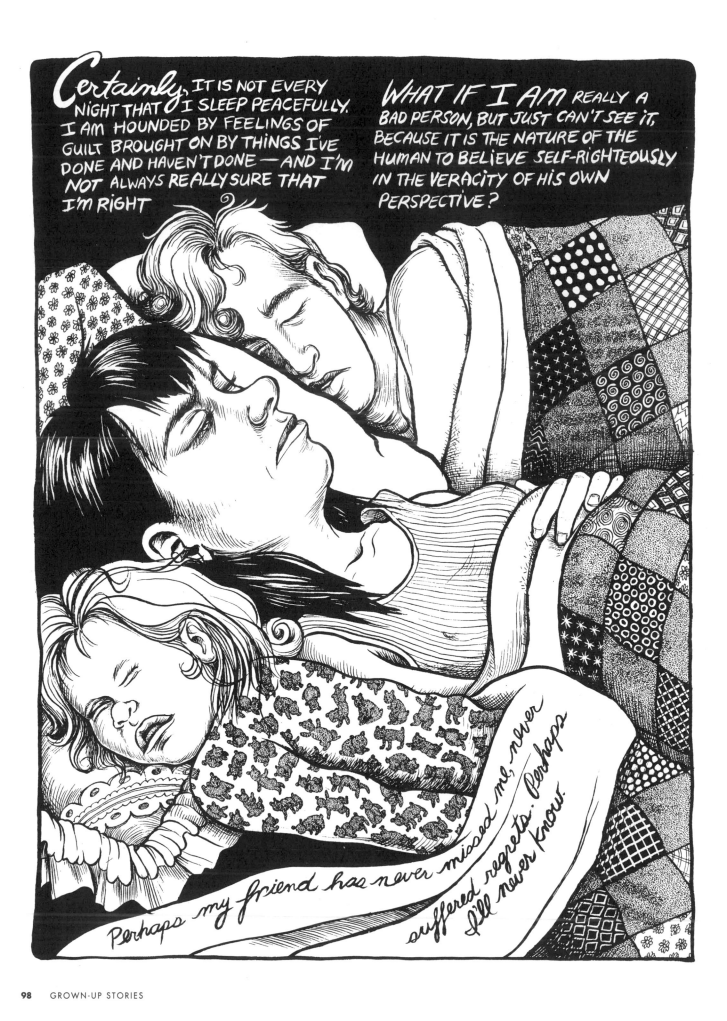

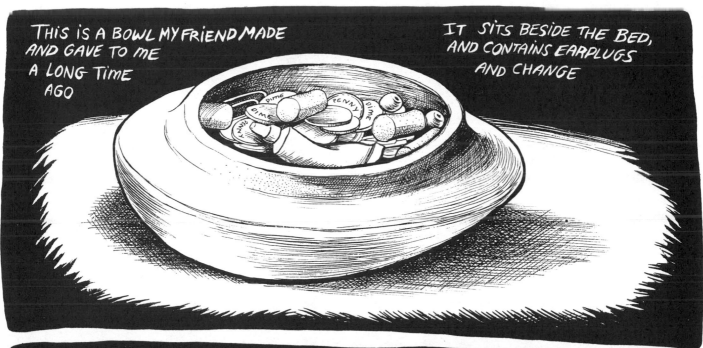

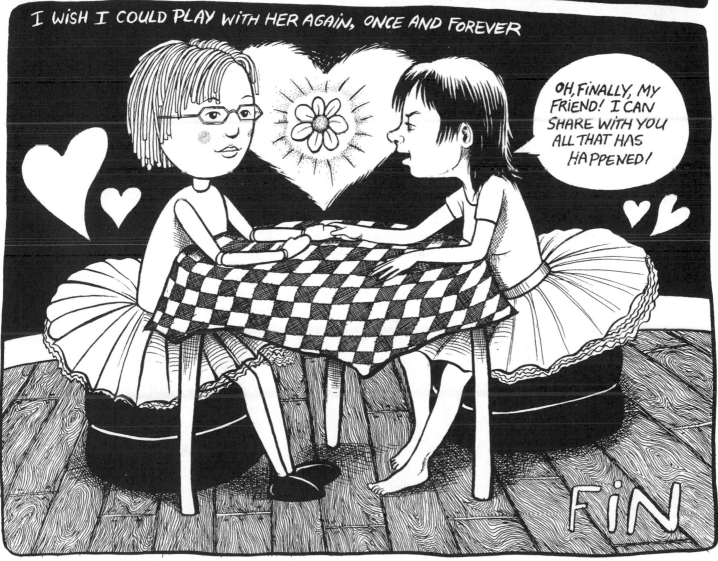

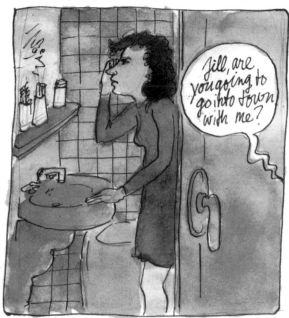

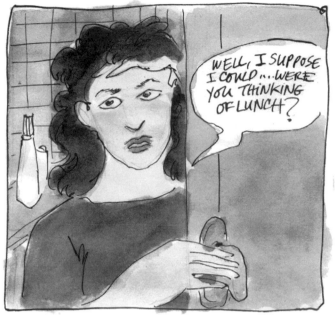

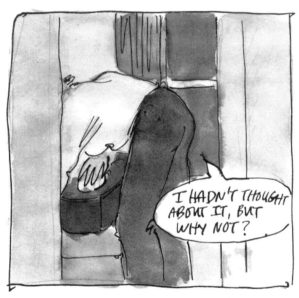

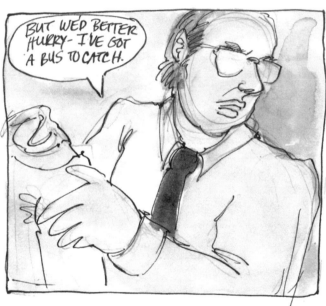

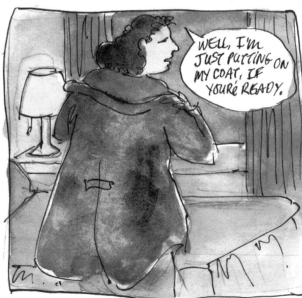

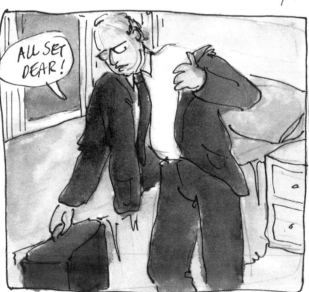

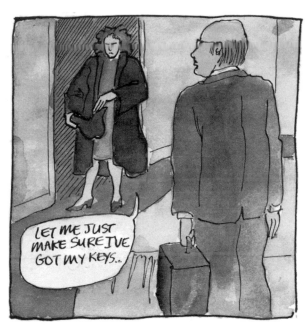

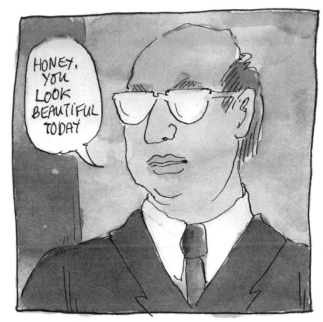

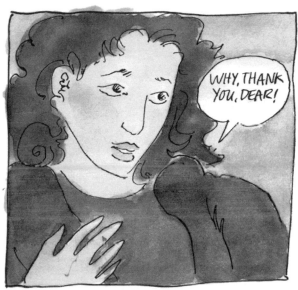

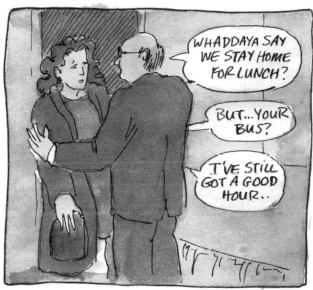

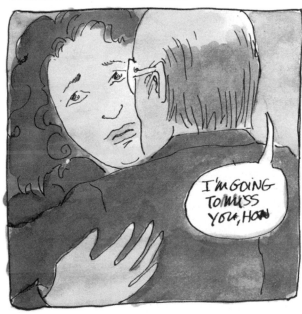

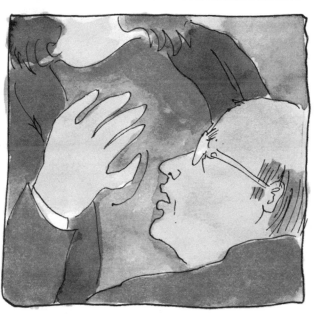

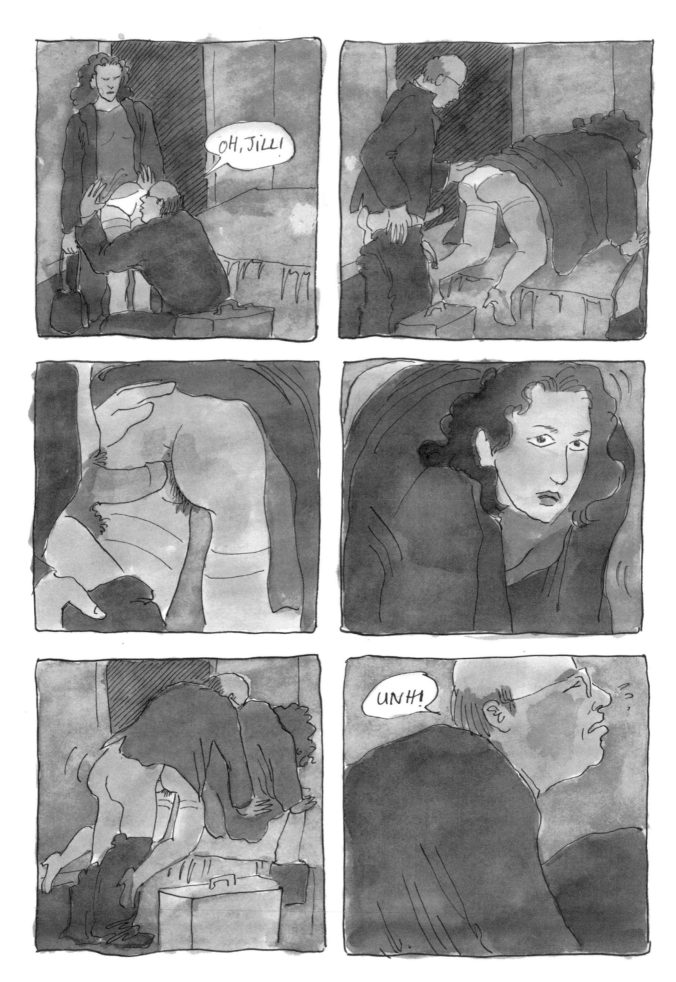

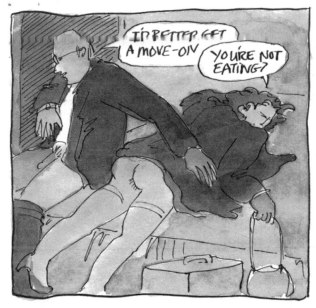

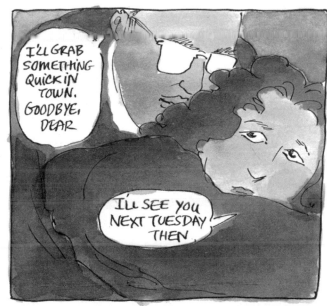

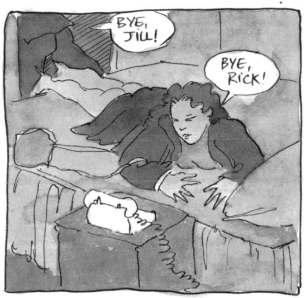

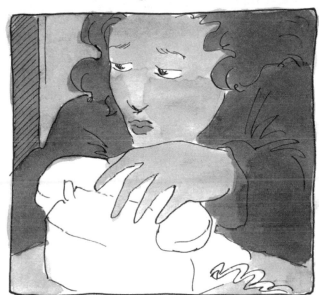

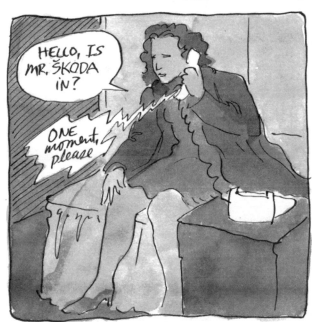

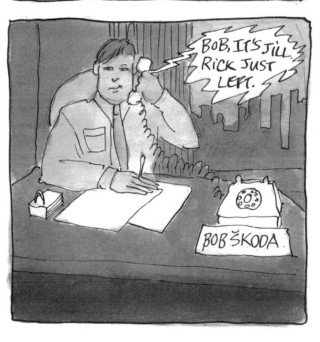

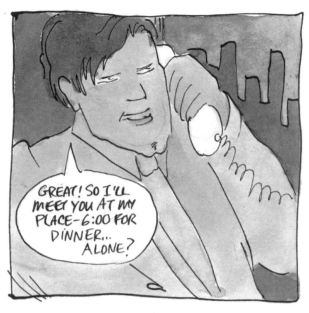

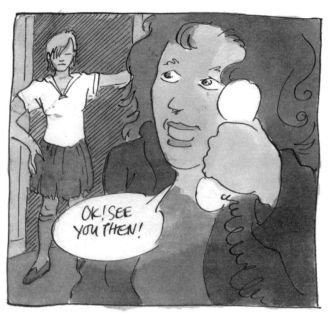

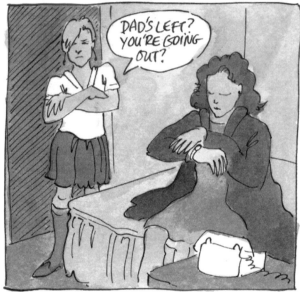

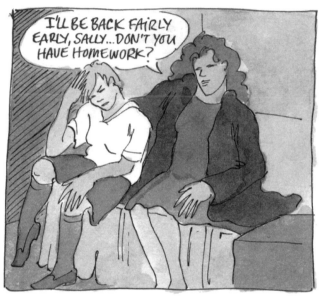

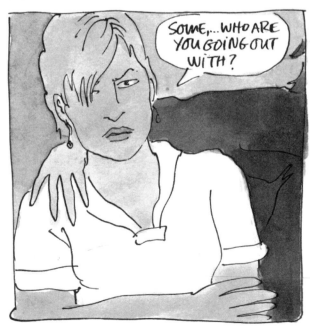

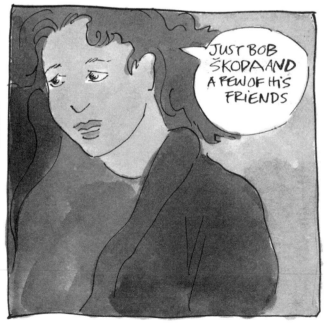

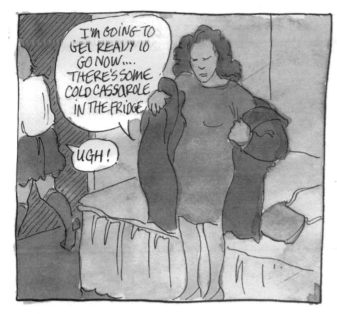

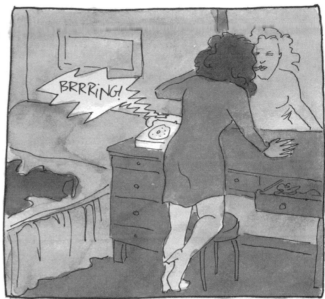

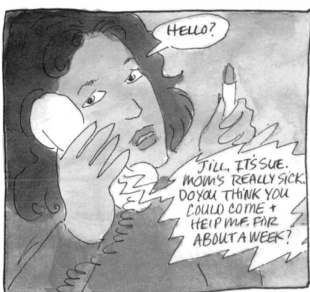

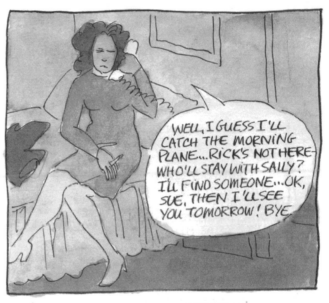

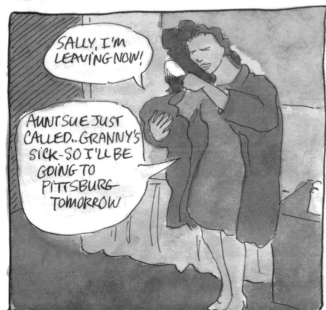

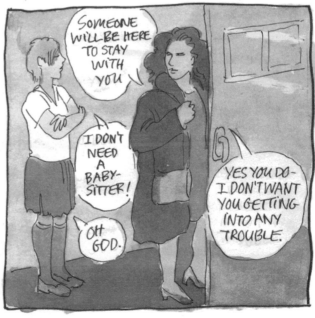

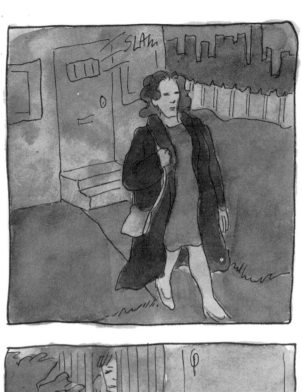
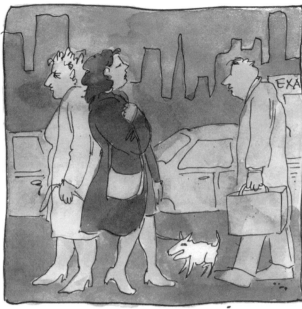
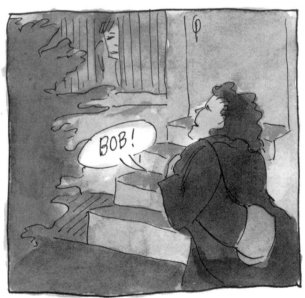
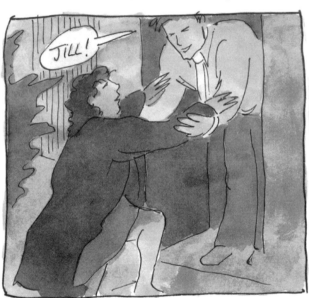
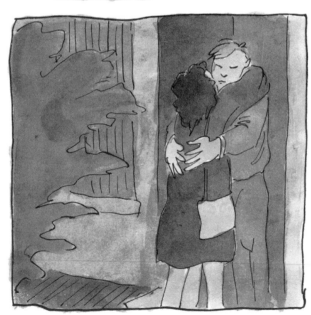
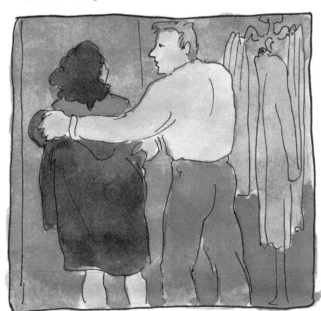

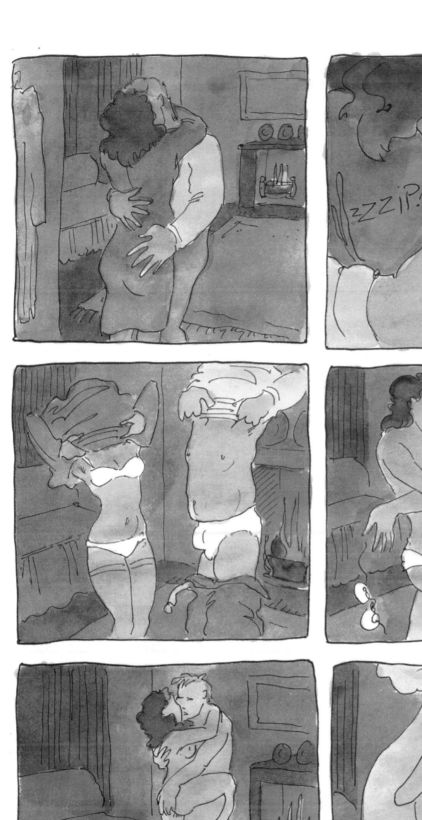
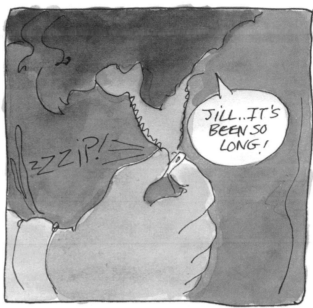
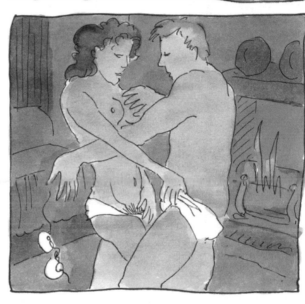
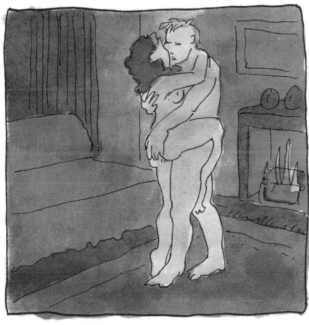
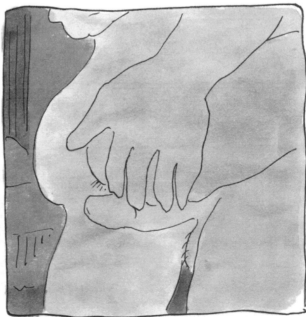

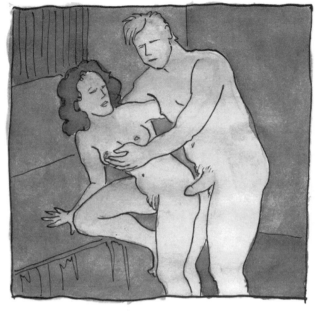
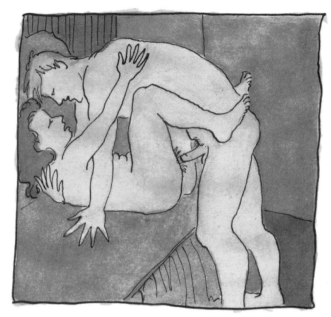
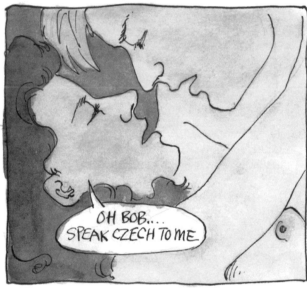
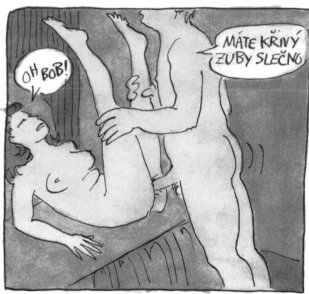
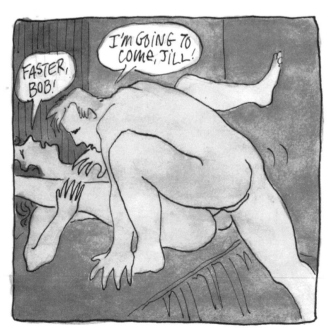
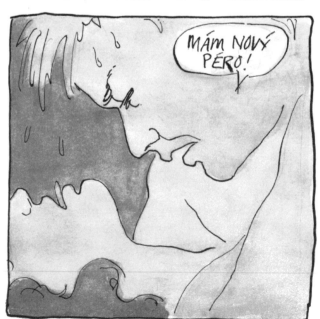

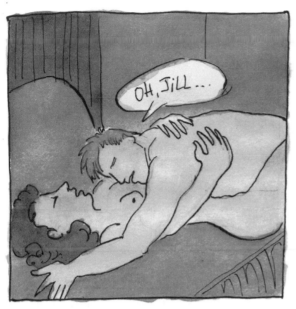

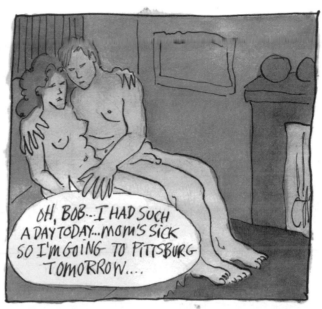

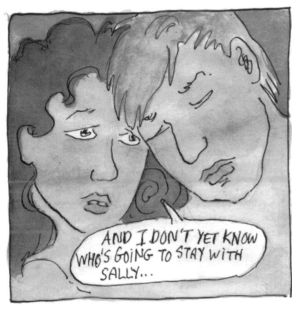

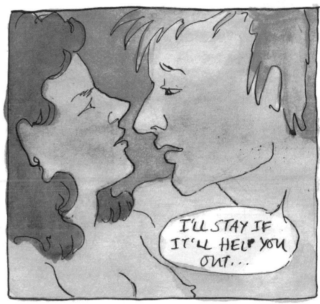

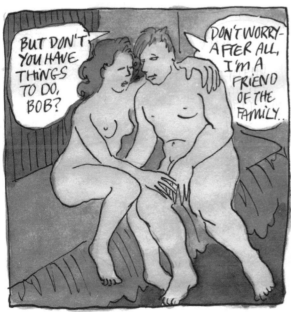

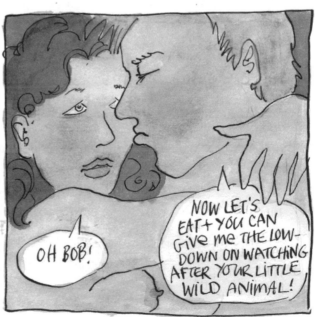

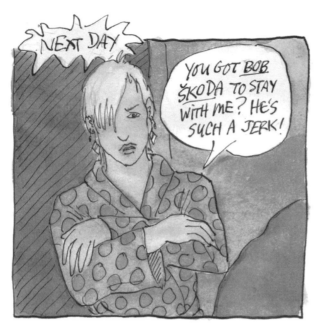

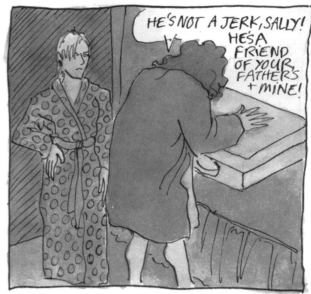

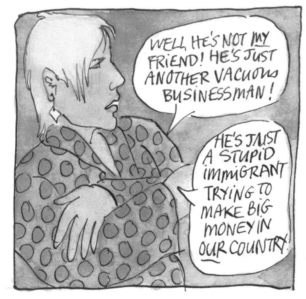

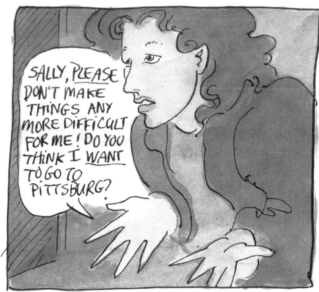

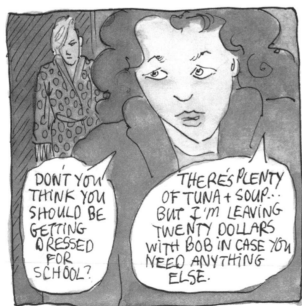

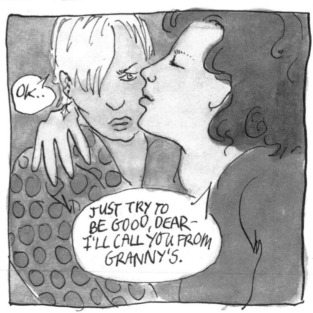

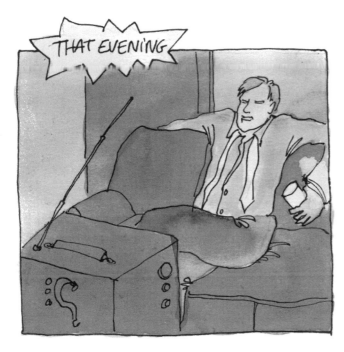

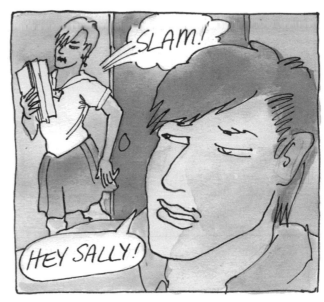

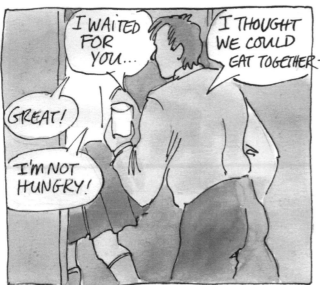

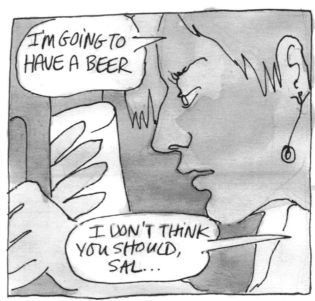

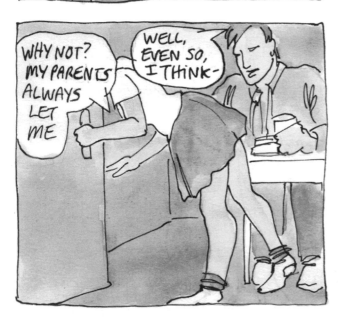

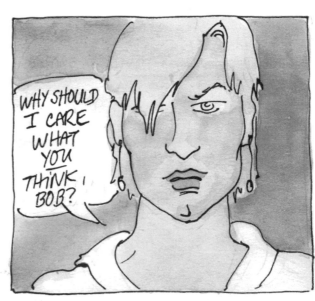

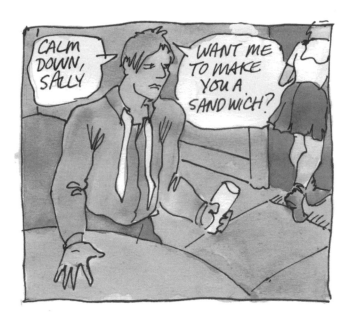

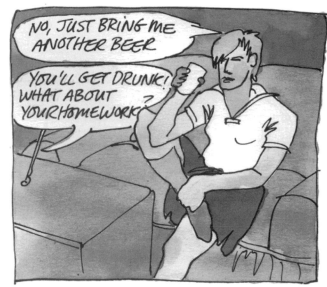

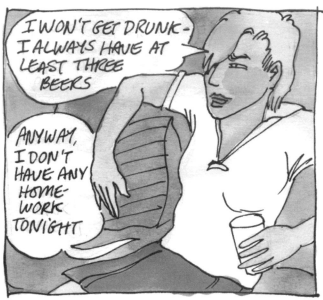

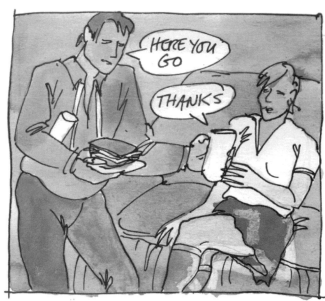

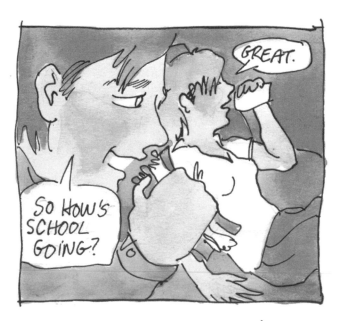

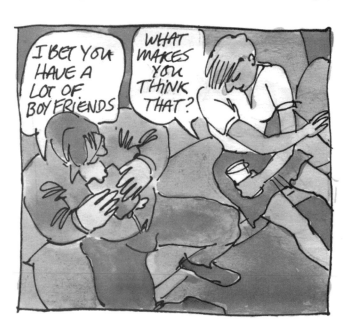

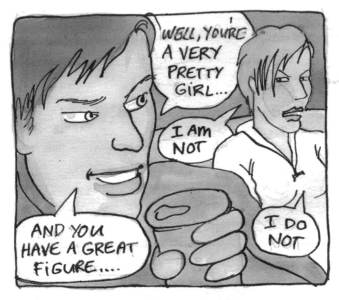

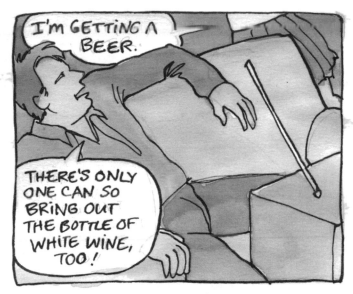

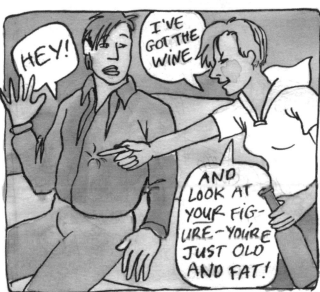

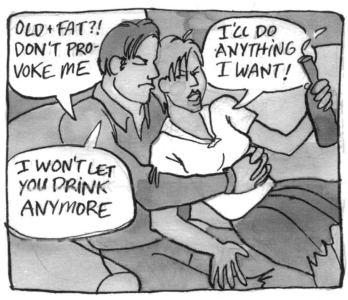

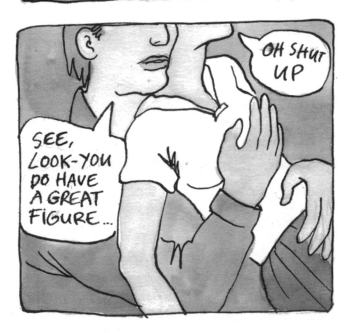

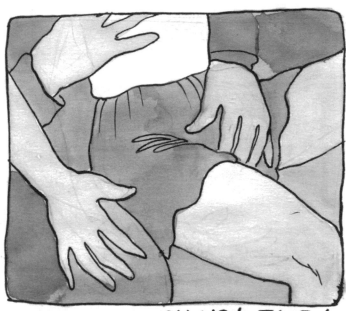

OH NO! END!

TIME OUT FOR PAIN three ¾ views by Phoebe Gloeckner ©'96

I NEVER EXPECTED TO BE HAPPY.

THAT'S NOT WHAT LIFE IS ABOUT.

THESE DAMN BLEEDING-HEART WIMPS WHO ALLOW THEMSELVES

THE LUXURY OF SUFFERING MAKE ME SICK.

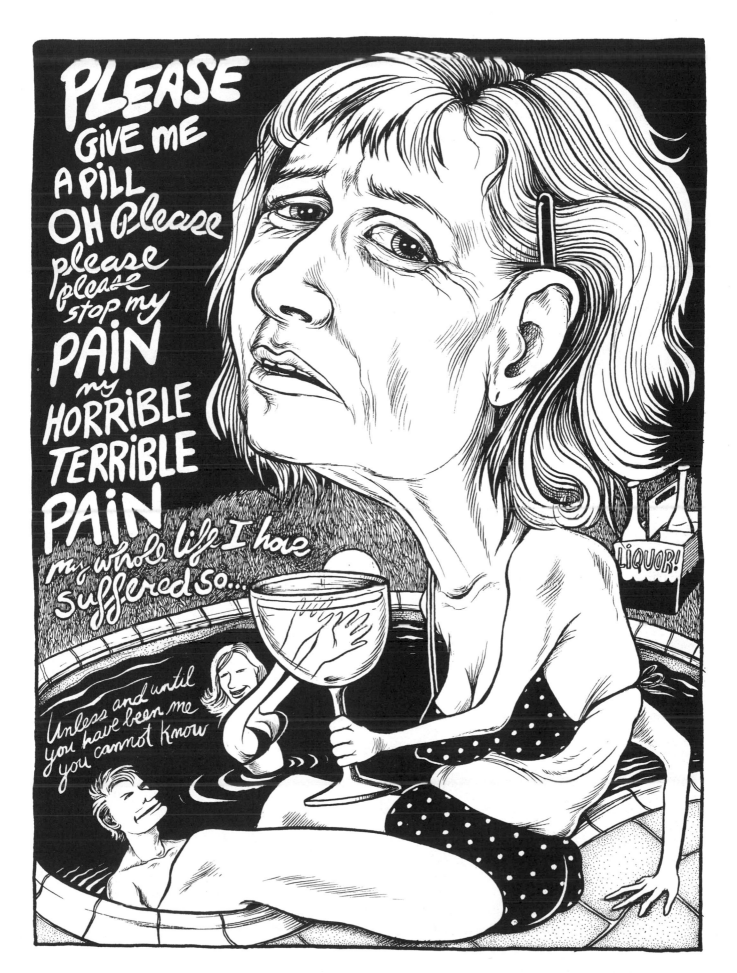

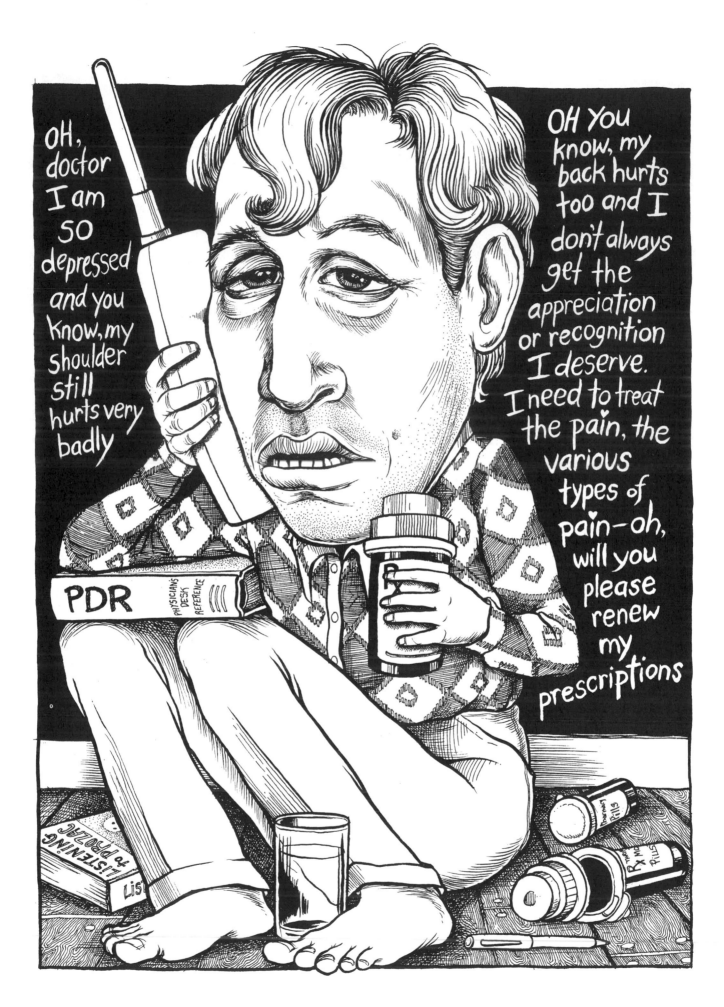

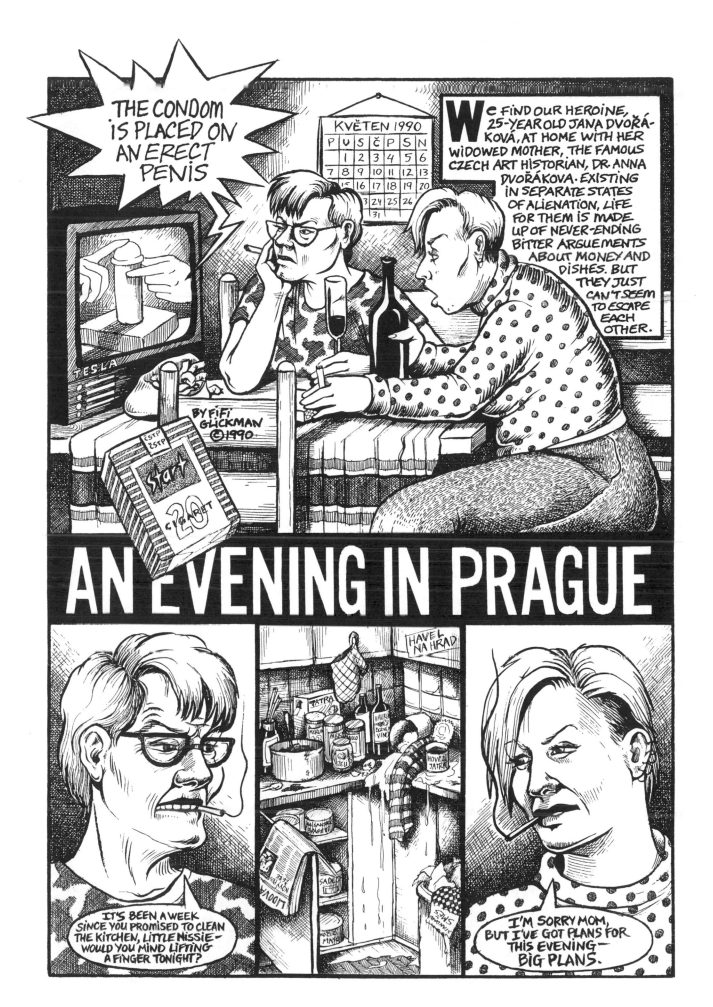

AN EVENING IN PRAGUE

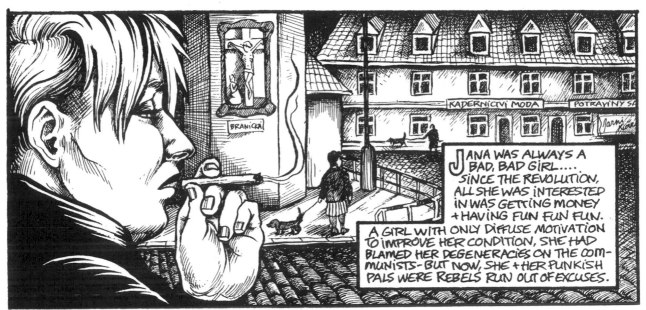

JANA WAS ALWAYS A BAD, BAD GIRL.... SINCE THE REVOLUTION, ALL SHE WAS INTERESTED IN WAS GETTING MONEY + HAVING FUN FUN FUN. A GIRL WITH ONLY DIFFUSE MOTIVATION TO IMPROVE HER CONDITION, SHE HAD BLAMED HER DEGENERACIES ON THE COMMUNISTS— BUT NOW, SHE + HER PUNKISH PALS WERE REBELS RUN OUT OF EXCUSES.

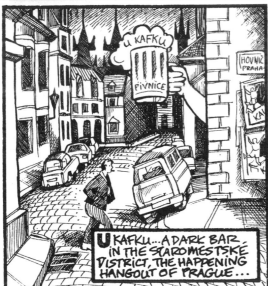

U KAFKU... A DARK BAR IN THE STAROMĚSTSKÉ DISTRICT, THE HAPPENING HANGOUT OF PRAGUE...

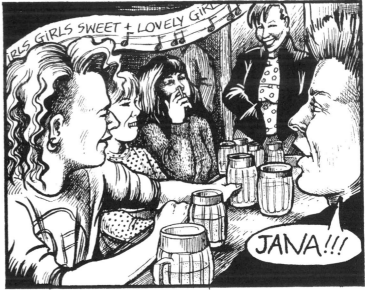

JANA!!!

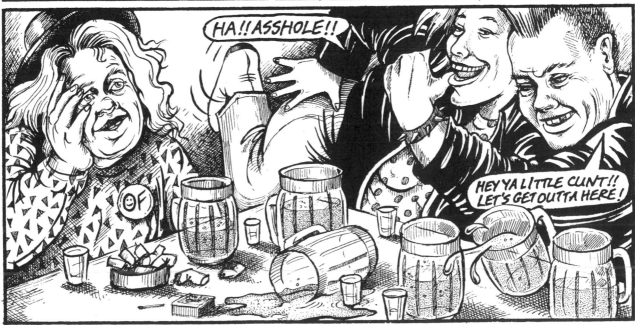

HA!! ASSHOLE!!

HEY YA LITTLE CUNT!! LET'S GET OUTTA HERE!

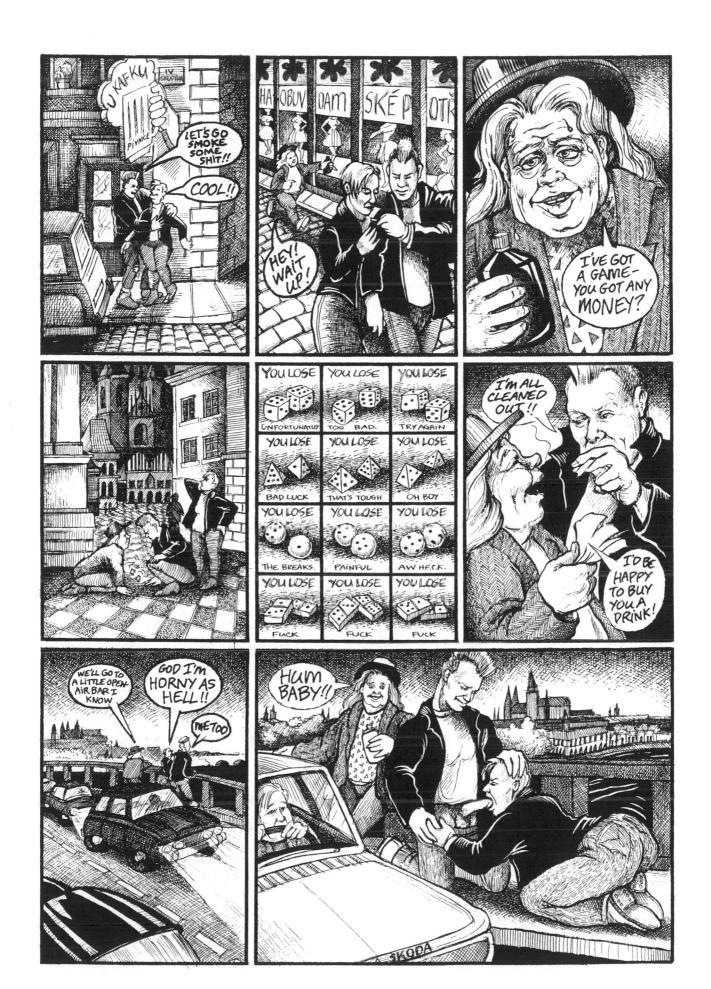

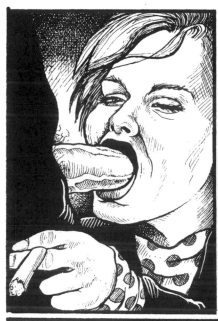

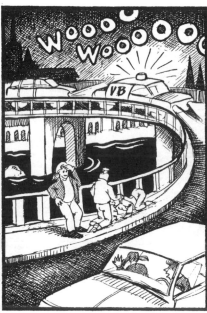

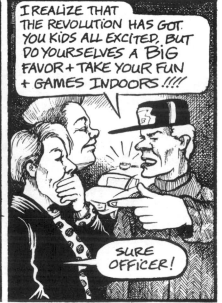

I REALIZE THAT THE REVOLUTION HAS GOT. YOU KIDS ALL EXCITED, BUT DO YOURSELVES A BIG FAVOR + TAKE YOUR FUN + GAMES INDOORS !!!!

SURE OFFICER!

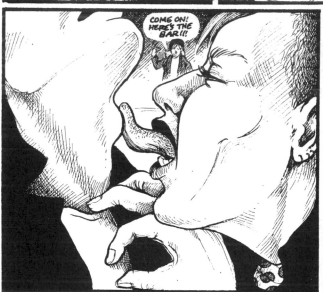

COME ON! HERE'S THE BAR!!!

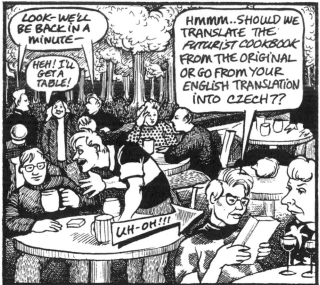

LOOK—WE'LL BE BACK IN A MINUTE—

HEH! I'LL GET A TABLE!

HMMM..SHOULD WE TRANSLATE THE FUTURIST COOKBOOK FROM THE ORIGINAL OR GO FROM YOUR ENGLISH TRANSLATION INTO CZECH?

UH-OH!!!

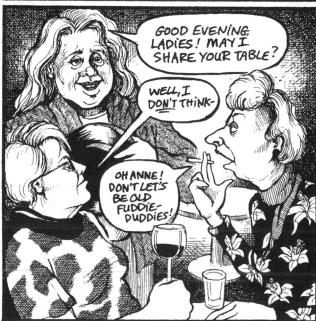

GOOD EVENING, LADIES! MAY I SHARE YOUR TABLE?

WELL, I DON'T THINK—

OH ANNE! DON'T LET'S BE OLD FUDDIE-DUDDIES!

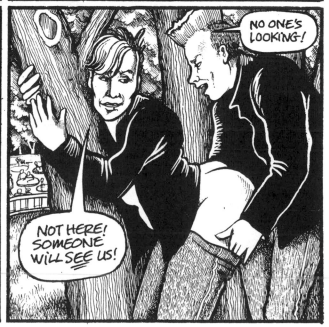

NO ONE'S LOOKING!

NOT HERE! SOMEONE WILL SEE US!

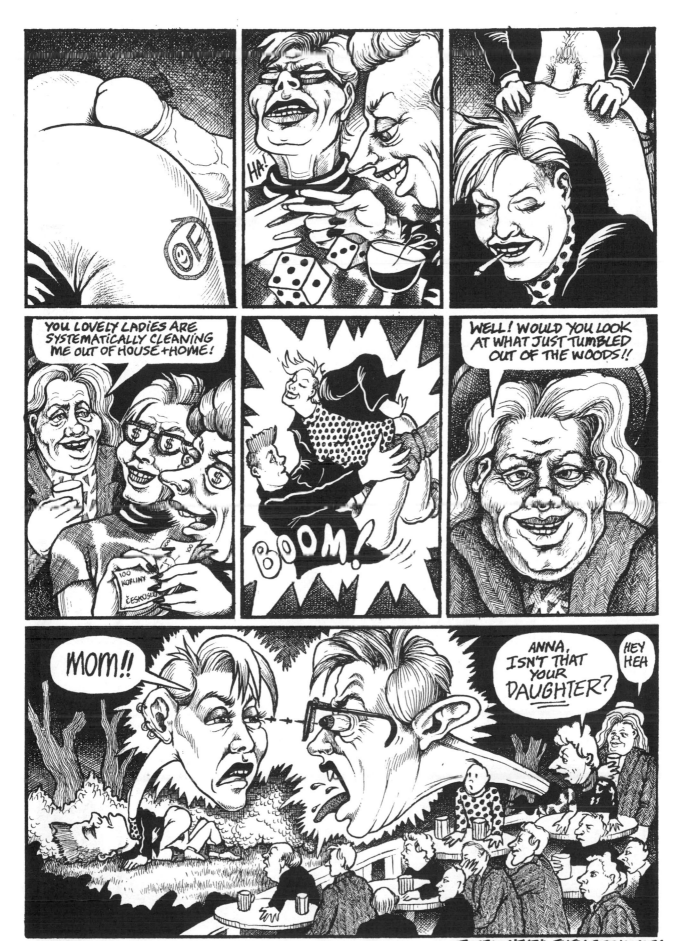

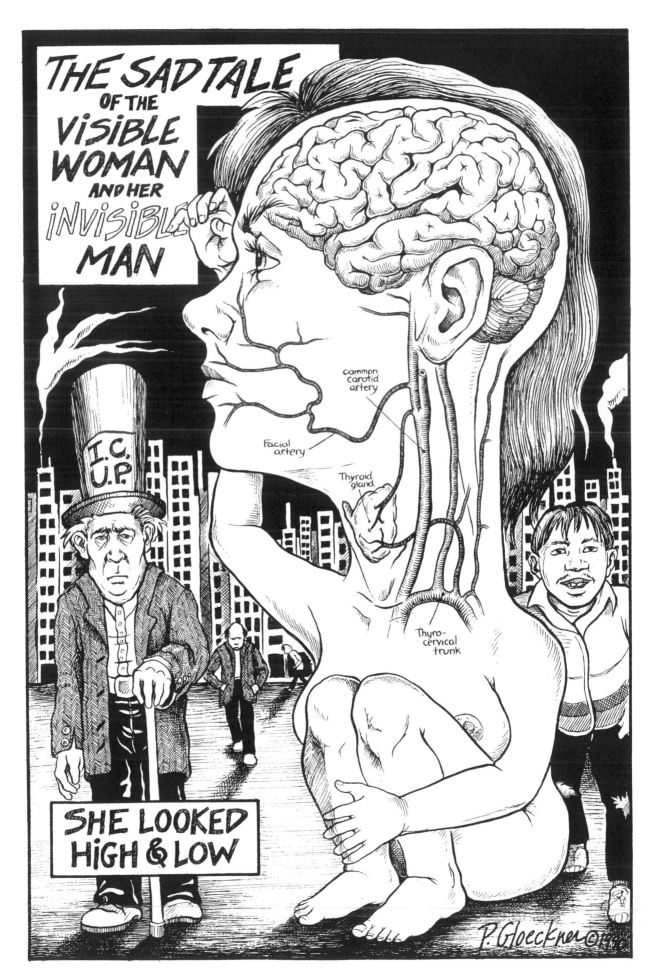

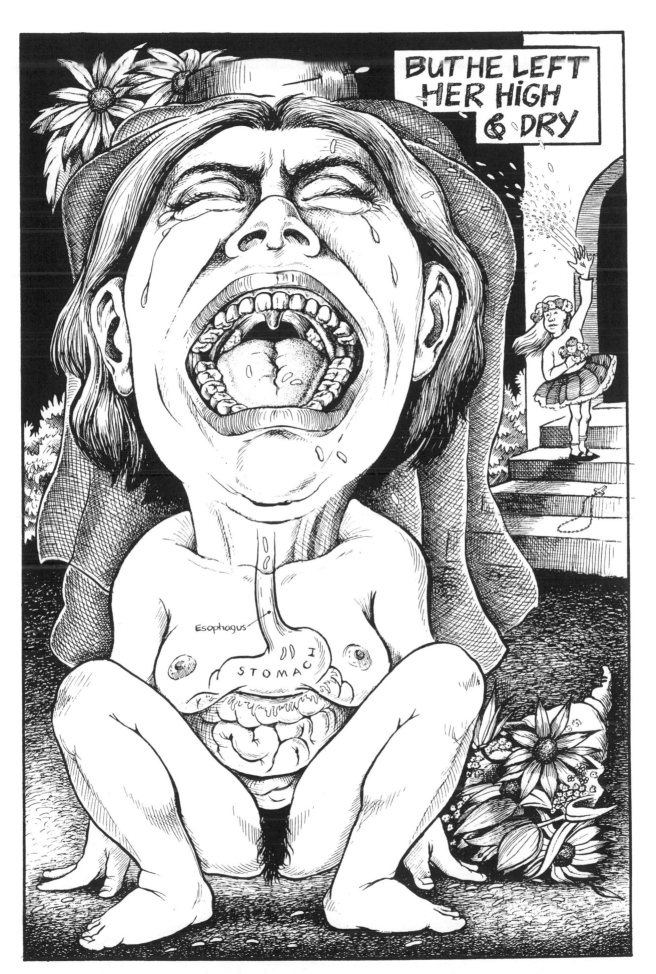

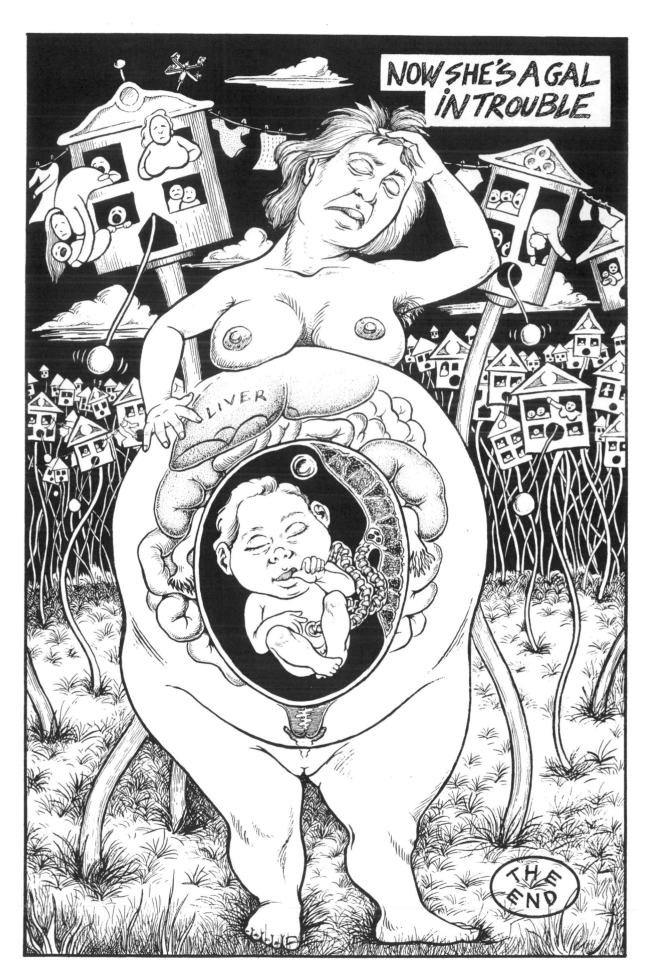

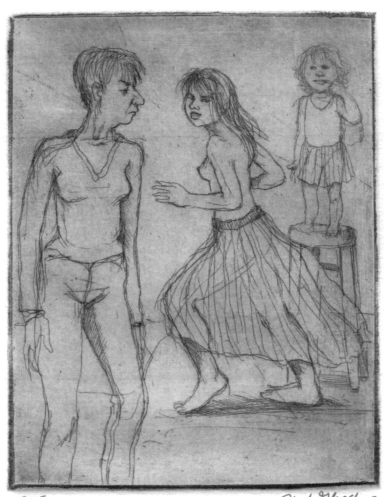

1995   *Phoebe Gloeckner*

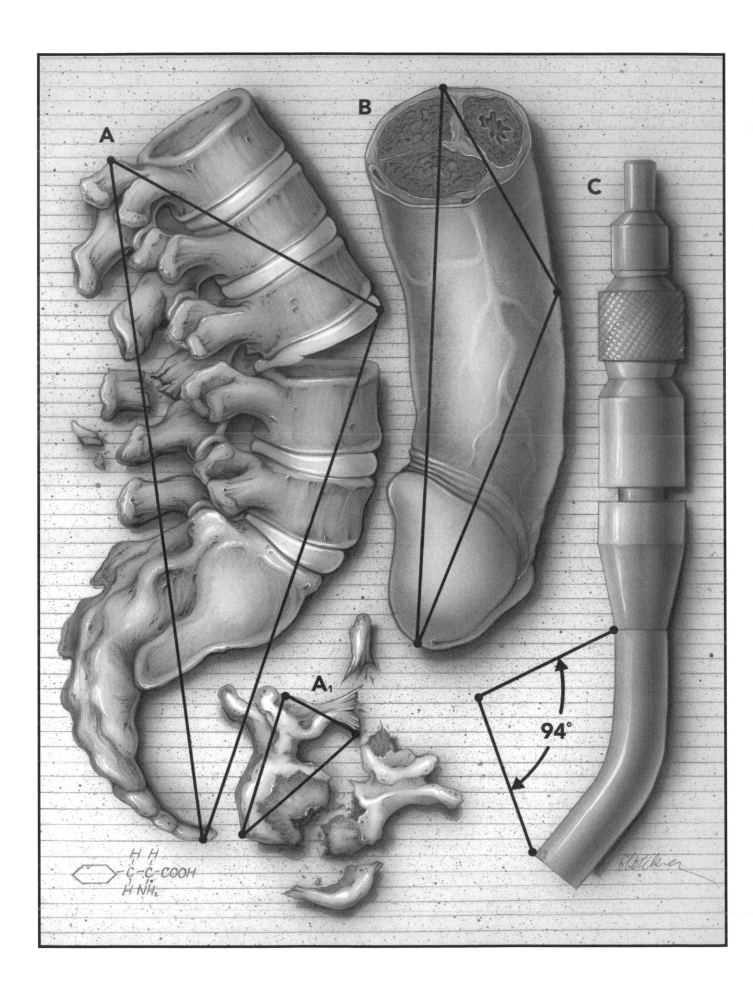

A

B

C

A₁

94°

H H
⬡—C—C—COOH
H NH₂

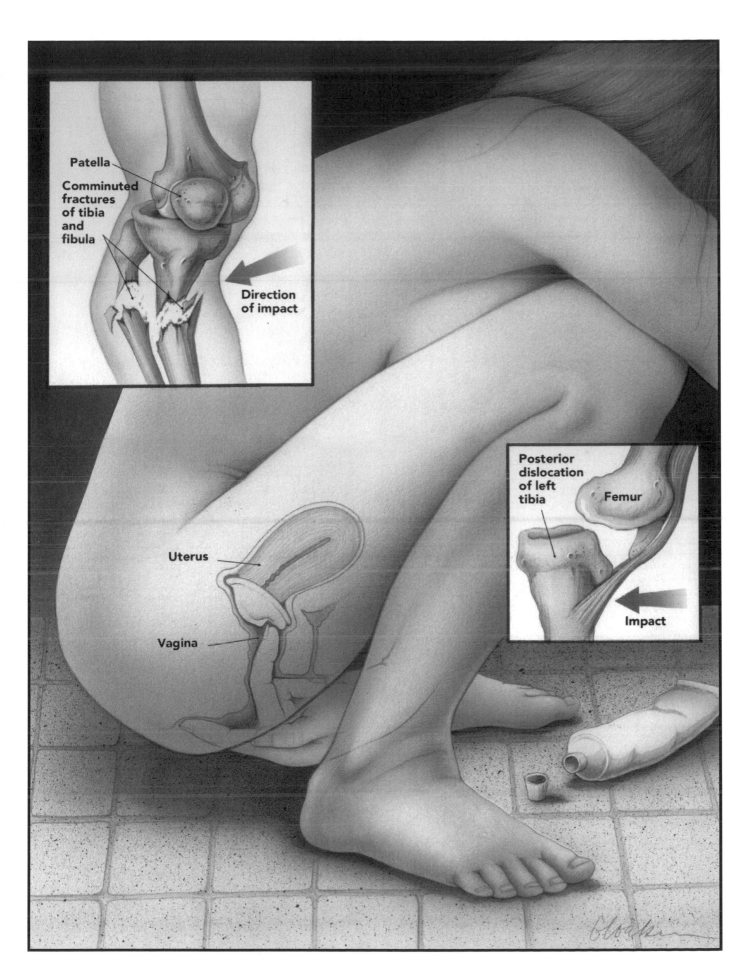

Patella

Comminuted fractures of tibia and fibula

Direction of impact

Posterior dislocation of left tibia

Femur

Impact

Uterus

Vagina

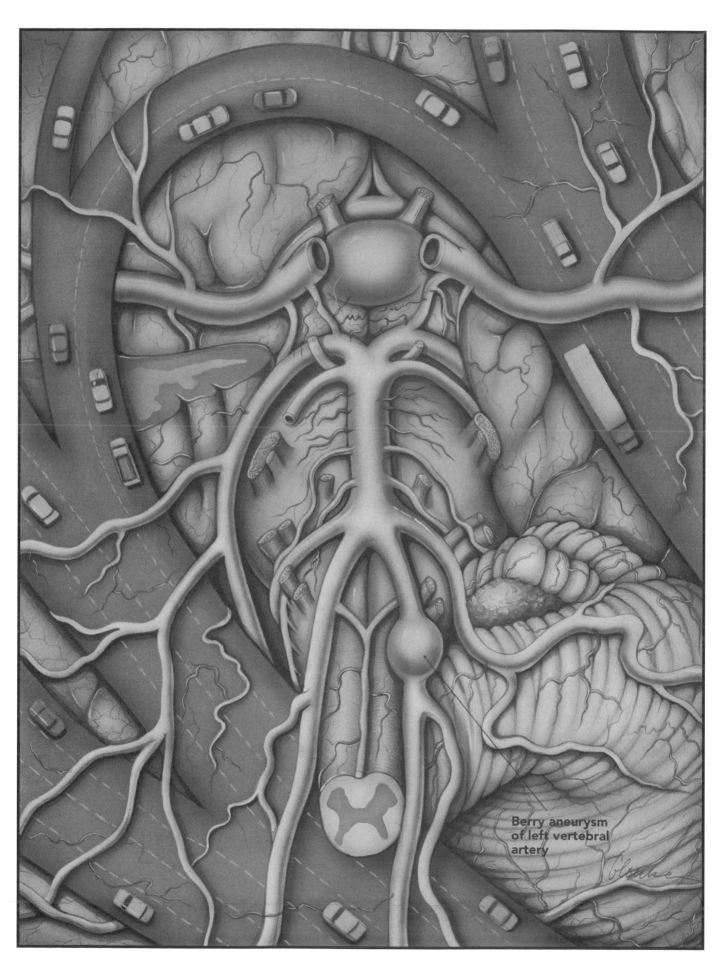

Berry aneurysm
of left vertebral
artery

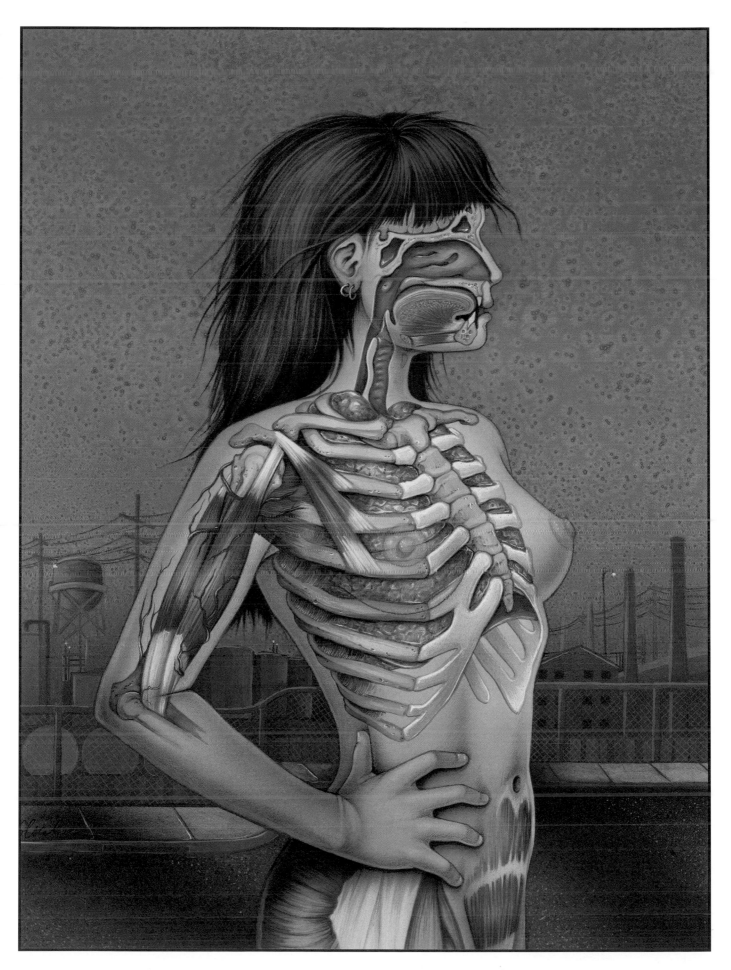

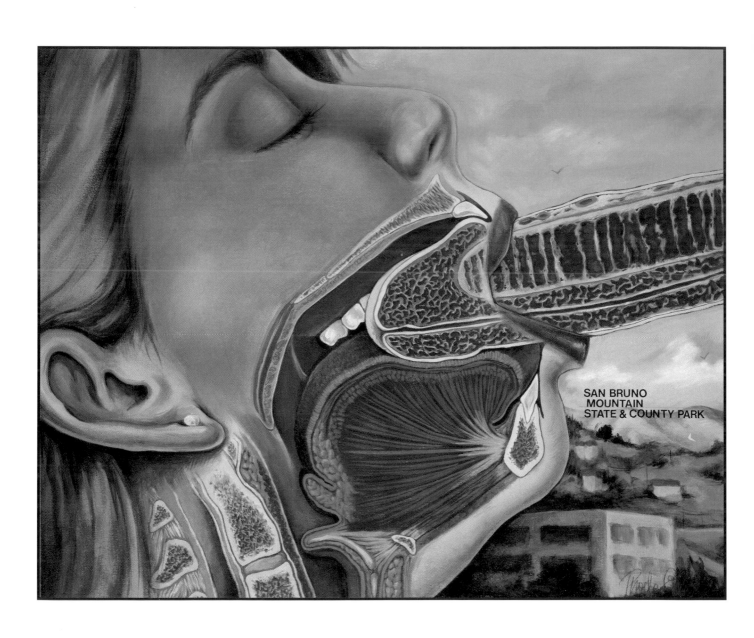

SAN BRUNO
MOUNTAIN
STATE & COUNTY PARK

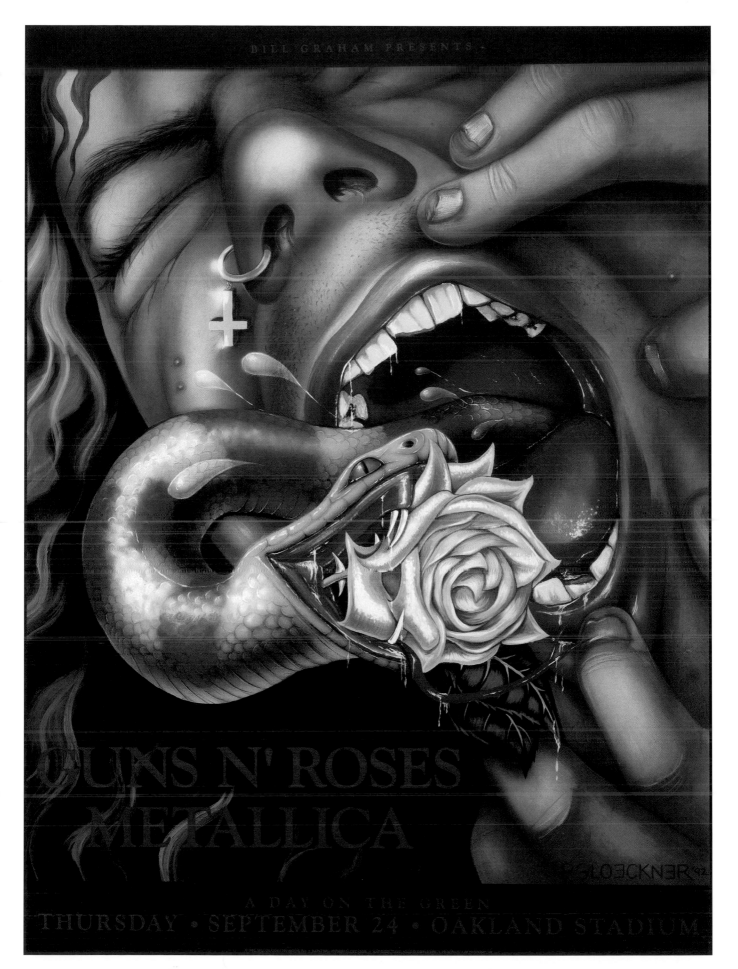

BILL GRAHAM PRESENTS

GUNS N' ROSES
METALLICA

GLOECKNER '92

A DAY ON THE GREEN
THURSDAY • SEPTEMBER 24 • OAKLAND STADIUM

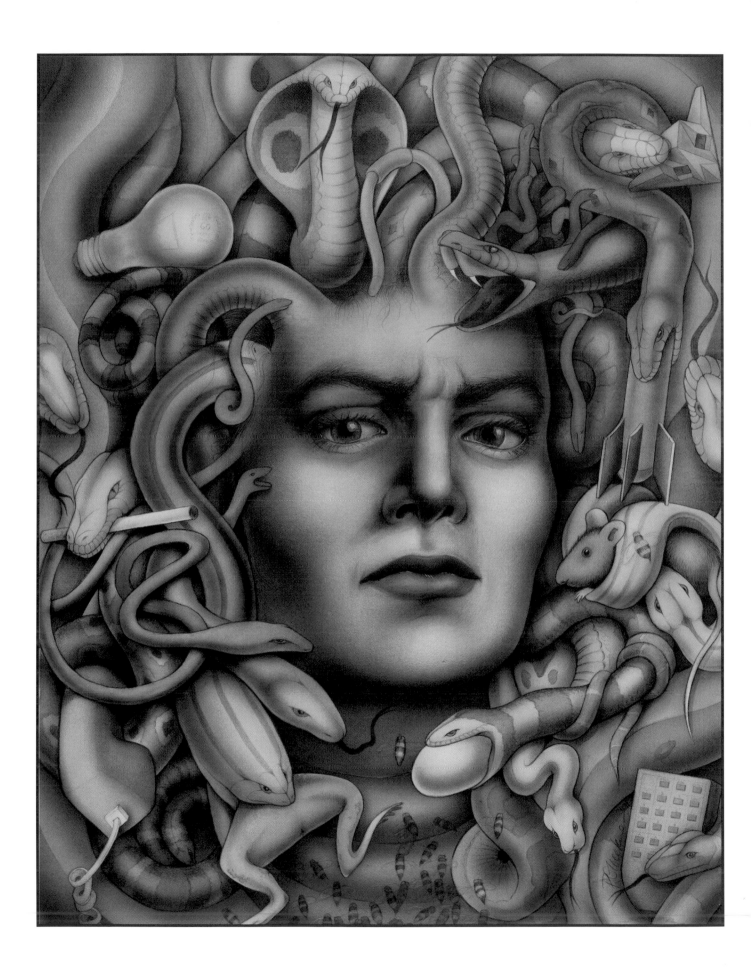

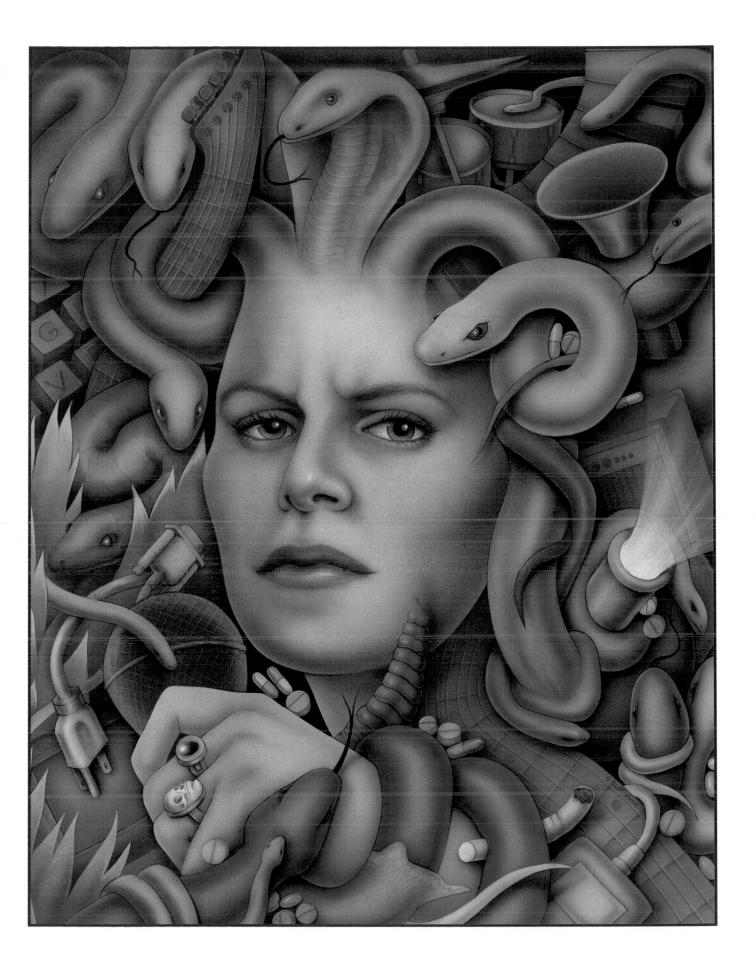

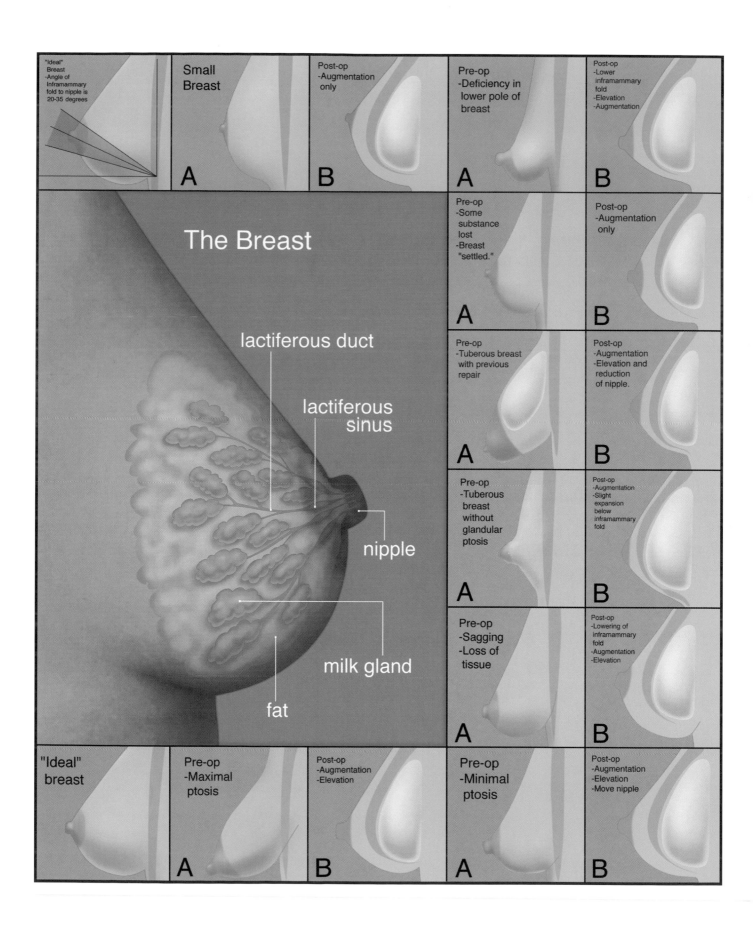

"Ideal" Breast
-Angle of Inframammary fold to nipple is 20-35 degrees

Small Breast
A

Post-op
-Augmentation only
B

Pre-op
-Deficiency in lower pole of breast
A

Post-op
-Lower inframammary fold
-Elevation
-Augmentation
B

The Breast

lactiferous duct

lactiferous sinus

nipple

milk gland

fat

Pre-op
-Some substance lost
-Breast "settled."
A

Post-op
-Augmentation only
B

Pre-op
-Tuberous breast with previous repair
A

Post-op
-Augmentation
-Elevation and reduction of nipple.
B

Pre-op
-Tuberous breast without glandular ptosis
A

Post-op
-Augmentation
-Slight expansion below inframammary fold
B

Pre-op
-Sagging
-Loss of tissue
A

Post-op
-Lowering of inframammary fold
-Augmentation
-Elevation
B

"Ideal" breast

Pre-op
-Maximal ptosis
A

Post-op
-Augmentation
-Elevation
B

Pre-op
-Minimal ptosis
A

Post-op
-Augmentation
-Elevation
-Move nipple
B

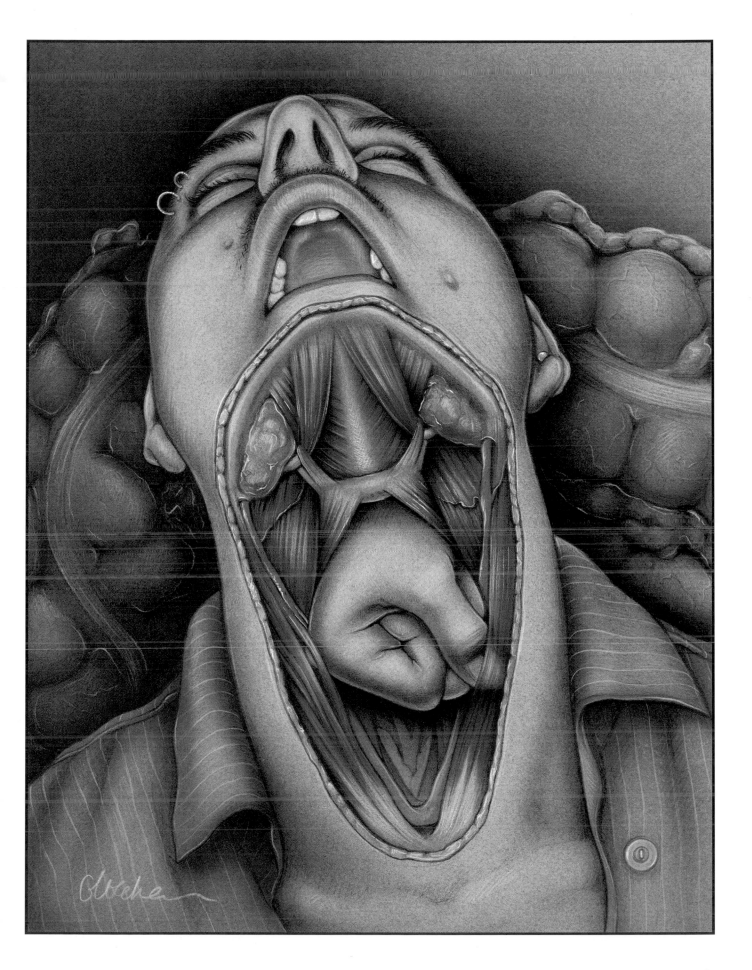

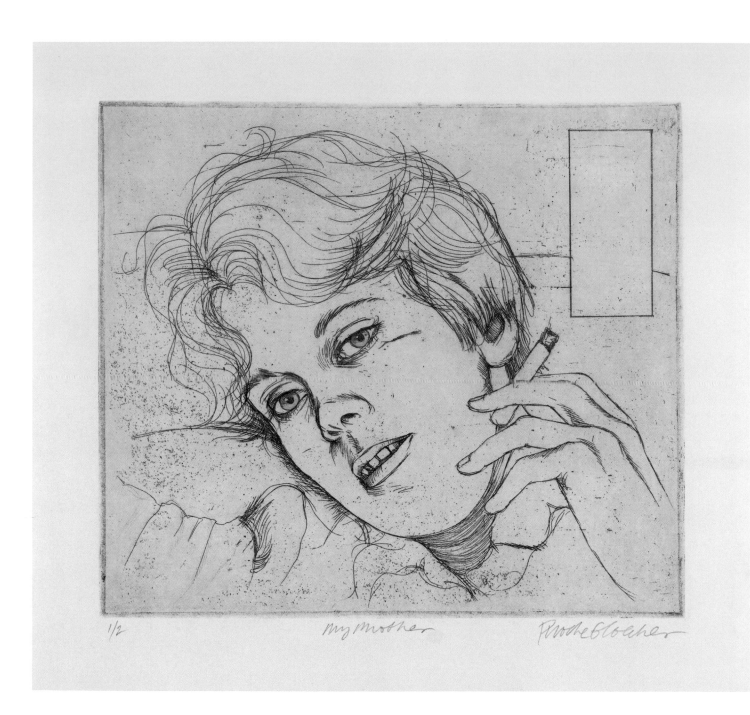

1/2   My Mother   Rhonde Glocher

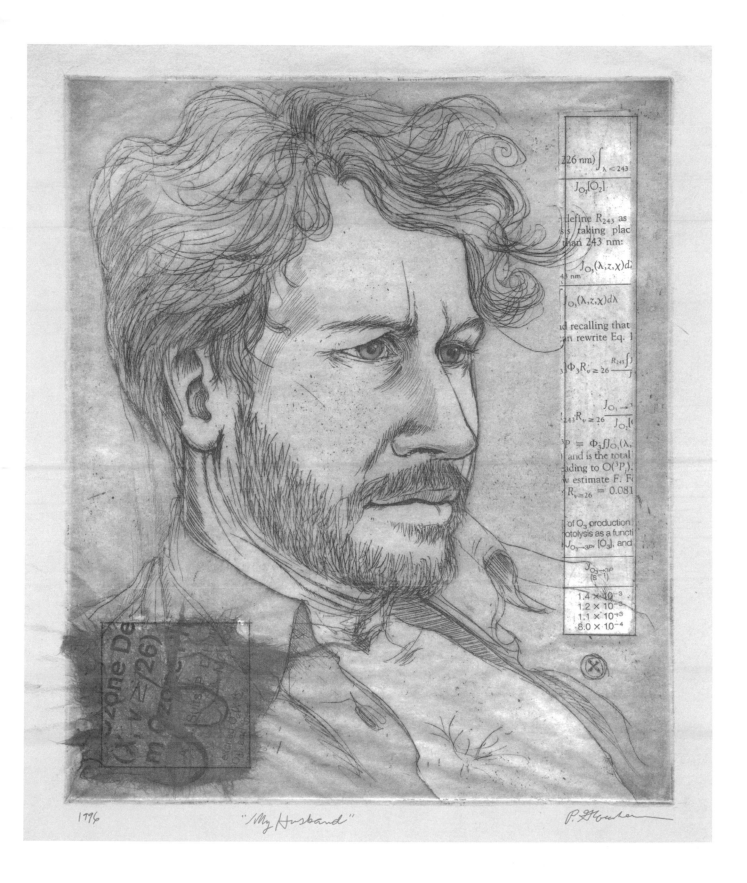

1996   "My Husband"   P. G. Booker

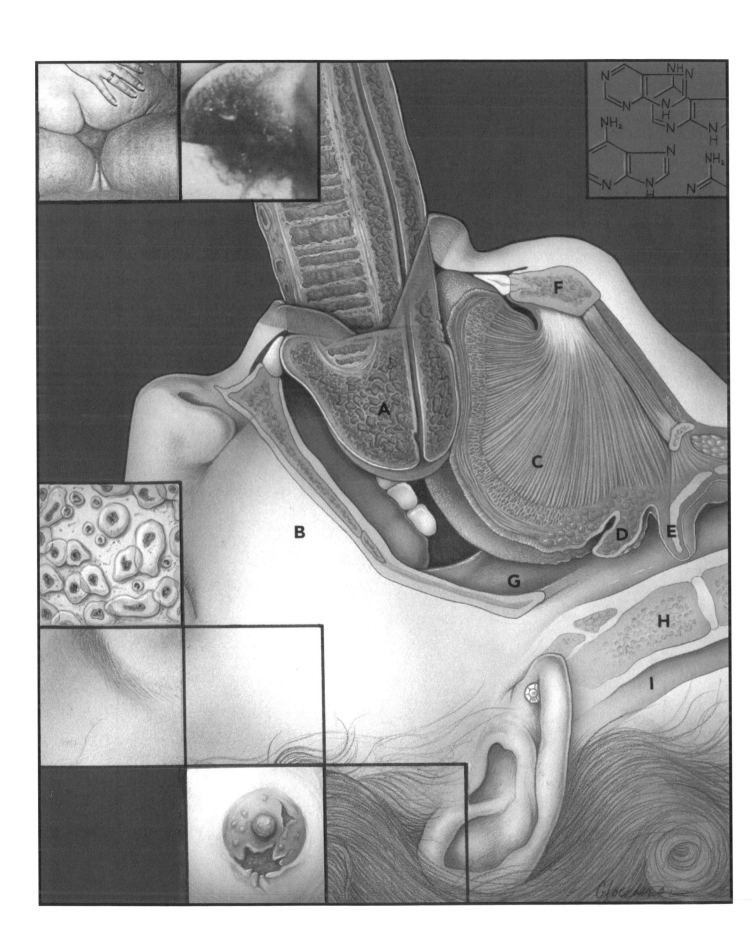

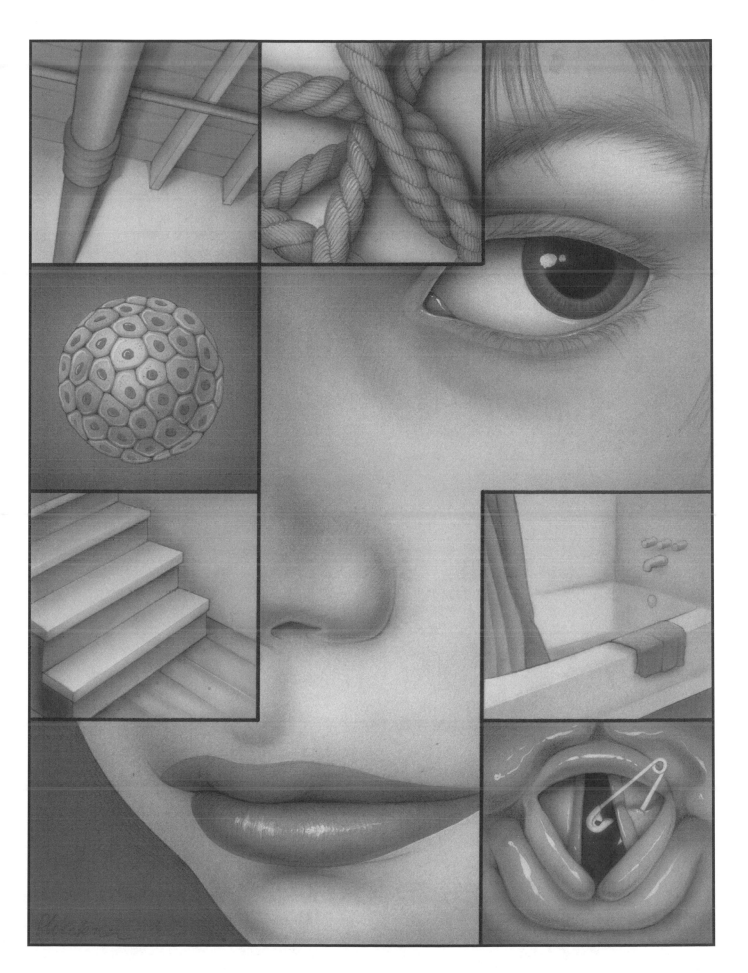

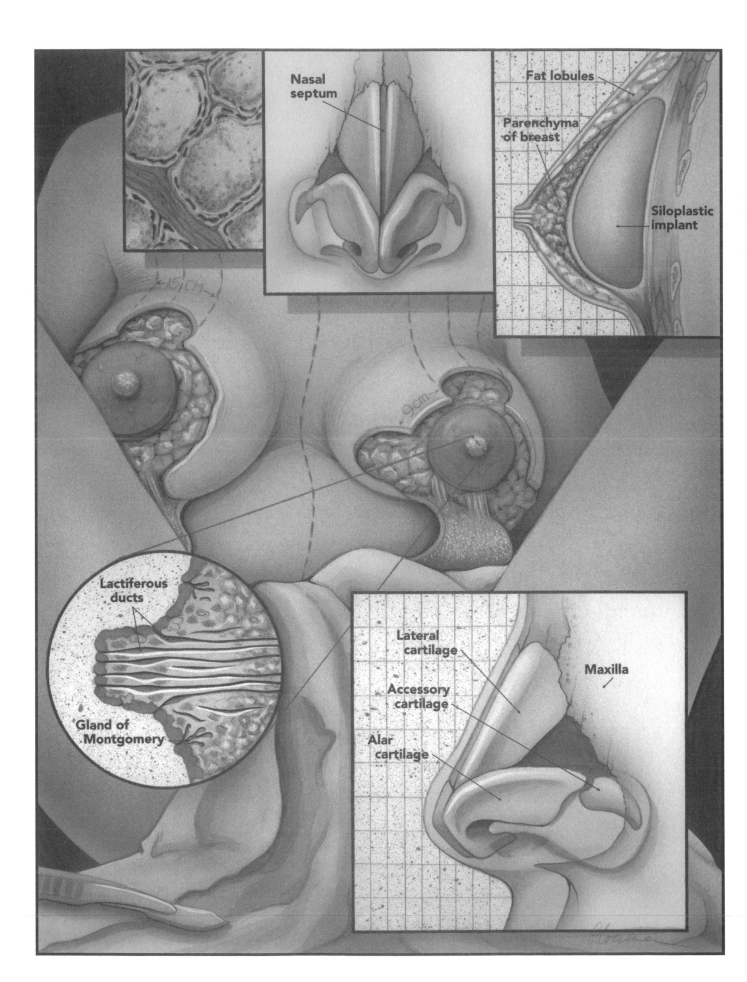

Nasal septum

Fat lobules

Parenchyma of breast

Siloplastic implant

Lactiferous ducts

Gland of Montgomery

Lateral cartilage

Accessory cartilage

Alar cartilage

Maxilla

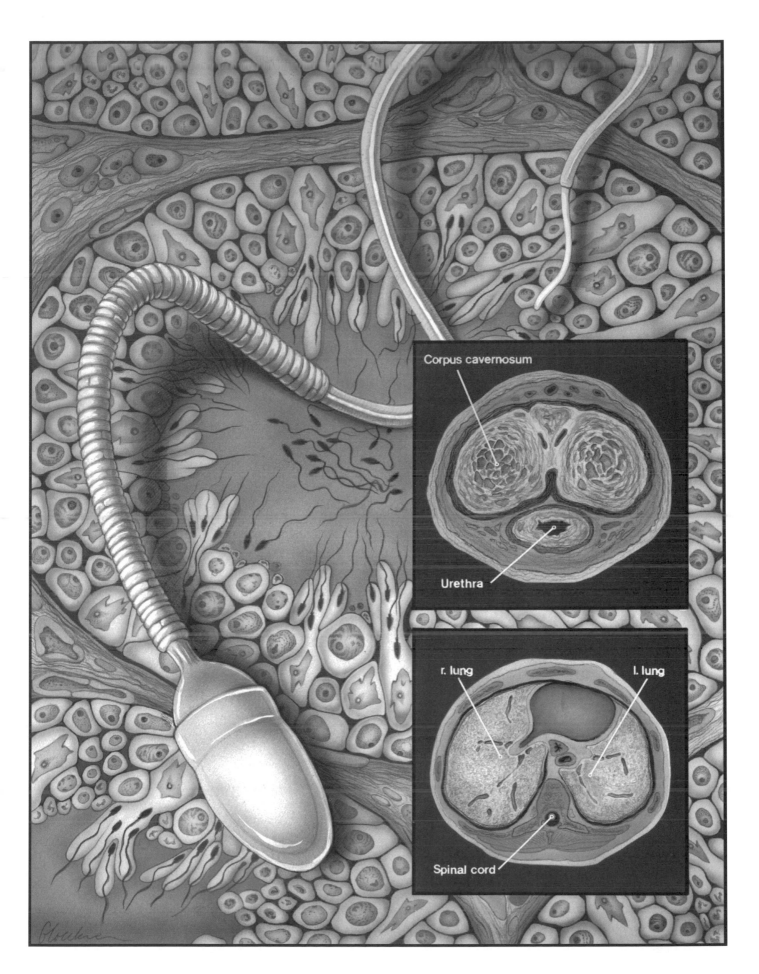

Corpus cavernosum

Urethra

r. lung

l. lung

Spinal cord

A Decorative Pair: "Desire Gratified"

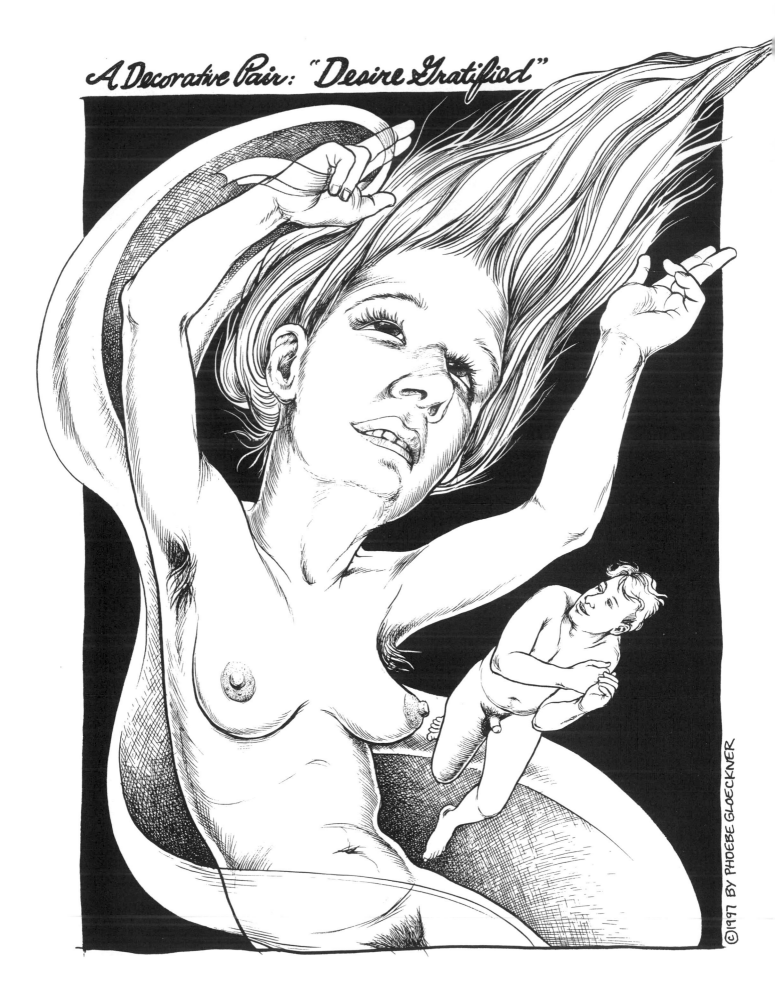

©1997 BY PHOEBE GLOECKNER

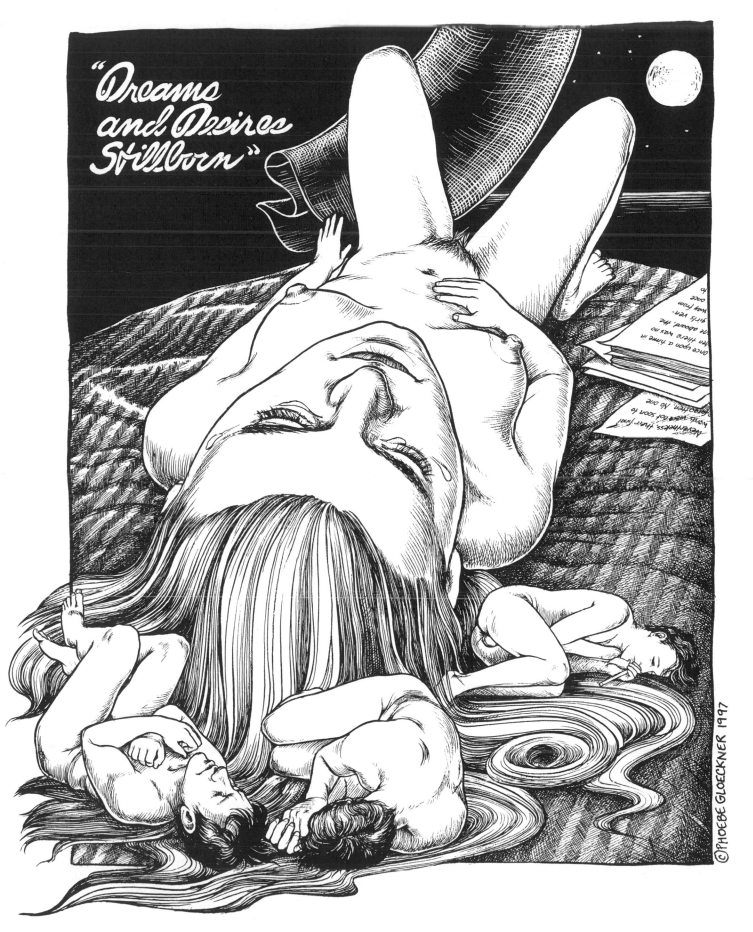

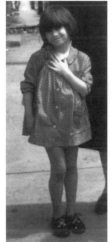

"little Phoebe," age five

Phoebe L. A. Gloeckner was born in Philadelphia, PA where she attended Quaker schools. At the age of twelve she moved to San Francisco, soon finding companionship and kindred spirits among the lost souls on Polk Street. She was expelled from many of the finest private high schools in the Bay area, ultimately completing her undergraduate studies in art and pre-med at San Francisco State University. She obtained an M.A. in Medical Illustration from The University of Texas Southwestern Medical Center at Dallas, in 1988. She has lived and studied in France and in Prague, as well as in the U.S.

She currently resides in Oakland, California with her husband, who is a scientist, and her six-year-old daughter.

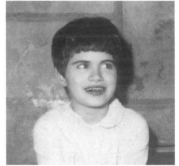

at age six

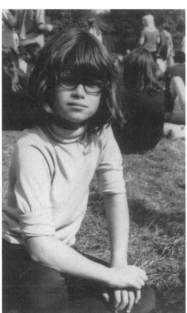

at age eight at a 1968 "be-in"

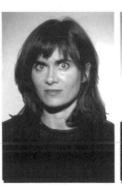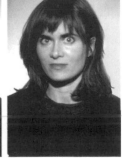

passport, 1998